© **Safari duha d.o.o.**
Translation and proofreading: Novellus prijevodi

Graphic design: Ivan Radić, Bsc. in Design and Professor of Visual Communications

Print: Graphic Institute of Croatia

The CIP record is available in the computer catalogue of the National University Library in Zagreb under the number: 001162368

ISBN 978-953-49043-5-0

Publisher: Safari duha d.o.o.
www.anabucevic.com

Life Is Beautiful When You Know How To Live It

Ana Bučević

To you, Marko,

with whom my soul, after a long journey, finally rests...

Chiara

Chiara was sitting on the bathroom floor, broken with grief and disappointment. She was completely devastated. Liam could clearly hear her sobs, but she didn't even try to suppress them.

"Chiara!", she heard Liam's voice coming from the other side of the door.

"Chiara, please open the door!"

She didn't hear him. She couldn't stop staring at the negative pregnancy test. The tears were pouring down her cheeks.

"Why? Why is this happening again? I can't cope with this any longer. I simply can't. My strength is abandoning me." She was saying these words in a low voice, in which a complete helplessness could be felt.

"What's wrong with me? Why me? Why did God choose to punish me?"

"Chiara, please let me in! Honey, please open the door!", she heard Liam's voice again.

She slowly got up and turned the key in the lock, without opening the door. She sat down on the floor, pushing her head deep into her knees, as if she didn't want to see the truth she had just witnessed.

Liam knelt down next to her and hugged her gently.

"Chiara, my love, it will work for us. I know we'll make it happen. We will not give up now. We have come a long way."

"Long way? We are at the very beginning. We haven't made one step forward, Liam!", she said through tears, but her voice was full of anger.

"One more negative test, that's how far we have come! I can't cope with this any longer. I simply can't. I can't go through this anxiety, waiting, hope, only to face disappointment over and over again. A disappointment that hurts even more with each new try. How long are we going to go through this, Liam? Forever? Perhaps I'm not worth enough to be someone's mum. God is obviously punishing me for the sins from my past. God knows that the biggest wish in my life is to have a child and be a mother. For me, the worst punishment would be if this wish of mine doesn't come true. Do you understand that my life is meaningless without a child in it?"

Liam was silent. He knew that every word he might say now could only make things worse.

He himself goes through internal struggles and different phases, from despair and helplessness to hope and elation.

God knows how many times he has asked himself why is this happening to them.

But he knows that this won't do any good to either of them. His decision was to support her in everything. He has decided to ignore his inner voices that keep breaking him. He just wanted to be there for her, as much as he can.

That's why he knew he should keep quiet now. Keep quiet and help her with his presence and understanding.

He sat on the floor next to her, and hugged her. His hug was gentle and strong at the same time, as if he was telling her to cry her soul out. He wanted to show her that he understood her and was there for her and that together they could make everything happen.

The next morning, Chiara got up later than usual. She barely slept. She spent the whole night sifting through her thoughts that were racing through her head.

She thought about the months and months of unsuccessful attempts to get pregnant.

Four years are behind them. Four years of disappointment. Forty-eight pregnancy tests. And all of them have turned out to be negative. All forty-eight of them!

Three attempts to get pregnant by artificial insemination. Trips to other countries, thousands and thousands of Euro spent. And what for? Just to stare at negative tests?! To be punished with sadness that just gets bigger and bigger with each failure?!

Last night she made the decision that she can't go on like this. Something has to change.

She knew that stress affects her and her body. She knew she had to stay as calm as possible.

She made coffee, sat in the garden and called Andrea.

Andrea was her best friend, whom she met three years ago at a conscious breathing course.

They clicked immediately.

Andrea was the complete opposite of her. Calm, positive, optimistic. Her life was perfect. She had a wonderful husband, a job she adored, a three-year-old son. She looked fantastic. She was bursting with energy and always had a smile that would light up any room she entered.

Chiara liked everything about this woman. A happy woman, who had a great life. She achieved everything she wanted in her life. She got everything she set her eyes on.

And that's what Chiara wanted, too. But, Chiara did not envy Andrea. Because she knew that she deserved all of it. Andrea could have told Chiara how to live her life, what she should change in her life, condemn her, but she has never done any of that. She has never experienced anything but pure understanding and friendship from Andrea.

Andrea lived her life to the fullest. And she was always telling Chiara: I live and let the others to be the observers of my life. Anyone who wants to learn how everything works for me will approach me and ask how.

"Hi, sweetie!", Andrea's voice was heard from the other side of the line.

"Hi, Andrea!", Chiara replied, trying to sound happy.

"How are you? Are there any news?", Andrea was curious.

"I'm not pregnant, Andrea. Another failure."

"Oh, sweetie!", enormous affection could be felt in Andrea's voice.

"How are you? How are you feeling? How is Liam?", Andrea continued with numerous questions.

"Terrible, Andrea! I just feel terrible! I am completely broken. You know that feeling when you lose all hope? When you feel like you don't have the strength to try again. That's how I'm feeling right now. I wasn't able to sleep the last night. I spent all night in tears. I'm empty and tired. I'm sure Liam feels the same way, but you know him. He loves me so much that he keeps putting his focus on me and my feelings. He didn't tell me anything, but I'm sure it's as hard for him as it is for me. What if he leaves me, Andrea? What if I become less of a woman for him with each negative test? He deserves to have a child, too. And I can't give it to him. What if it finally gets to his head? That he will never be complete with me?"

Now she could barely talk. She was choking in tears.

"I'm coming over. I'll be there in fifteen minutes", Andrea said, quietly.

Chiara remained sitting in the garden, alone with her thoughts.

"I'm here!", she heard Andrea's voice, as she was opening the gate.

Chiara put a smile on her face and rushed into her friend's arms. She hugged Andrea firmly, as if she was thanking her for

15

coming.

"My dear, sweet Chiara!", Andrea addressed her, pulling her even tighter in her hug.

"All shall be well, you'll see. I know it, I feel it. You will hold your baby in your arms."

Chiara felt warmth and softness permeating her whole body, not knowing whether it was from the beautiful spring sun that broke through the clouds at that moment or from the very thought of Andrea's words.

"Come, sit down! Coffee is waiting for you."

"Tell me everything, my dear. I'm listening to you", said Andrea, looking warmly into her eyes and holding her hand.

"I'm exhausted, Andrea, completely exhausted. I've never felt worse than this time. You know how many times Liam and I have been through this, but this seems to be the end of the road for me. It was as if all my ships had sunk. As if hope and faith had completely left my body. I feel nothing but emptiness. Complete emptiness."

"I believe you, sweetie! You know how much I love you and how I'm always telling you that you are a lioness. Because you are, Chiara. Only strong women can endure what you are going through. And you are that kind of a woman. And it is quite normal to feel tired. And exhausted. This, what you are going through, requires strong mental strength. This is not just a physical process. This is also a psychological process. Even greater than the physical one."

"Well, that's what it's all about. About my head. I'd better not tell you about the thoughts racing through my head the last night. Horror. Nothing makes sense to me. Last night, I went through all the possible scenarios: That Liam had left me, found a new woman with whom he has children, and I was left alone, no one wanted me, everyone around me was happy, with perfect families, and I was alone, abandoned, unaccomplished... Horror movie. Which I will experience, as it seems to me. Everything is pointing to that direction. Everything! Why, Andrea? Why do all the other women manage to get pregnant, many of them even when they don't want to?! And I am deprived of a child by God. Me, who wants a child more than anything in my life and who would subordinate my life to being someone's mum, who would focus only on that child and give all of me to be someone's mum? You succeeded from the first try, too. Am I a worse person than you?"

"Of course, you're not, Chiara, but you know what I believe. My faith in how life is meant to be and how we should live it is my biggest guiding star. You know how much I believe in who we really are and that we are able to create our own reality. I've told you about it numerous times. How it is possible to change your reality and manifest what you want. Even when the things seem impossible to you. Especially then."

"I know. You have been telling me this. Maybe I wasn't able to hear you. But I need to change something. It doesn't work like this. Perhaps I should try that creation of yours? How, Andrea?

17

How do you do that? Do you want to teach me?"

"How is it done?", Andrea heard the most beautiful question she could hear from her friend. Because now she is ready. Now she will finally be able to hear her.

"But, of course! Let me immediately show you the power of our thoughts so that you immediately understand how our emotions are managed by us, not by external situations and events. And our thoughts cause our vibration and what we shall manifest in our lives."

"Let's do it", Chiara said readily. "What do I have to do?"

"Just answer the questions I'm going to ask you now."

Chiara settled down more comfortably, exhaling deeply, as if, with that exhale of hers, she was telling Andrea she was ready.

"Take a look at how you feel now", Andrea began in a low tone. "Describe your feelings now, at this very moment."

"I feel helpless. Sad and empty. Hopeless. As if I were a failure. I'm scared because it seems to me now that the future won't be the way I want it to be. I feel awful. In one word, awful."

"Do you know why you feel that way?"

"Because the test turned out to be negative the last night."

"That's not the real reason, Chiara. If it was because of that, you would feel like this every time the test was negative, and you didn't, right?"

"I didn't, but it wasn't the forty-eighth test in a row. It's not the same to see the first test negative, the tenth or the forty-eighth."

"It's the same, if you understand what it is that makes a difference in people."

"How is it the same? How can it be the same to see a negative test for the first time or go through this bad experience for the forty-eighth time, after four years of trying, waiting, hoping?"

"How do you know that it was the forty-eighth test in a row?"

Chiara gave her a look full of disbelief.

"What do you mean? How do I know it's the forty-eighth test in a row?! What kind of question is that?!"

"Just trust me and you will understand everything pretty soon. Just answer me: How do you know that this was the forty-eighth test in a row?"

"Well, I can count, Andrea! We have been trying to have a baby for four years. I take a test every month. This is the forty-eighth test I've made so far. That's how I know. I know how many times I have experienced disappointment. I also know what clothes I was wearing each time I took the test. Everything is still clearly present in my head. All the pain after each test. And that's why I feel worse than ever. I have experienced disappointment so many times and now, when I saw the test again, I've remembered all those times until now, when I thought it would work, it would finally work. But, instead of that, I've got negative results again."

"Exactly. The point of my question is hidden in your answer. It wasn't the negative test that caused you this feeling, but you, going back in time, to all those failed attempts before. To all the negative tests, all the disappointments so far."

"I don't understand."

"If you had stayed the last night in the present moment without going into the past, and probably into the future, which you now doubt even more, you would have seen only a negative test. But, the last night, all forty-eight negative tests came back to you. Right?"

"Of course! The forty-eighth test in a row! How can I not know how many tests I've taken?!"

"It's not the point that you don't know. It's not possible for you not to know this. The point is not to go back to those moments because it will not lead you to your goal. In the moment of current failure, going back to all previous failures won't do you any good. Failure is the path to success. These are all current situations that are not and do not have to be permanent. It's very important how you perceive it. Do things happen to us that we don't want? Yes! Does it have to be like this forever? No! This is exactly where the key difference between people hides. It is possible for you to learn to look at the test and feel sadness and disappointment, but those feelings can last very shortly and you will be able to move towards your goal, no matter which test in a row it was."

Andrea continued: "Did you know that the author of the world's best-selling self-help book, Jack Canfield, was rejected by fourteen publishers before being accepted by one. Fourteen! How many people do you think would have given up by then? How many people would knock on the door of fourteen publishers? If Jack had said that this was the fourteenth publisher he had approached, he would have never taken that step and knocked on one more door. And that last time was decisive. Do you understand what I'm trying to tell you? In order to reach the goal, we need to focus on the goal and not on the obstacles. Chiara, do you know who succeeds in life? Those who don't give up! That is the only real success. But people always see the end result, and they think it was achieved overnight. It's not true! Every success, seemingly achieved overnight, started years earlier."

"And what am I supposed to do, when I'm tired? What am I supposed to do, when I really have no more strength?"

"Find it in yourself, dear. You have it, just like all those who once thought they didn't have it. There are the tools intended to bring out that incredible strength that every human carries inside. Take a rest first. It's okay to feel tired. We can't go anywhere when we are tired. Take a rest. Stop for a few days and allow yourself to take a break. Be proud of yourself, Chiara. That's a huge difference, compared to the feeling of guilt that is overwhelming you right now. People who climb the highest mountain peaks know that they don't need to walk for hours and days without stopping. They also stop and rest in order to gather strength to continue. It's okay not to be okay. And as soon as you accept this, you will feel better. It is the struggle that robs us of our strength. Struggle with ourselves. We get angry with ourselves, blame ourselves, even insult ourselves as incompetent, losers, worthless, etc. All this is additionally exhausting our spirit, which is what we need the most on our journey to success. And it is the mind that either strengthens or exhausts the spirit."

Chiara took another deep breath. But it was a sigh of relief this time. It was as if her friend had given her permission to indulge her feelings. It's okay to feel tired and sad.

"My dear Chiara, you will have a nice rest for a few days, and then you will start doing something that I will now teach you. Have you heard of visualization?"

"Yes, I have. They were also mentioning it on the course where we met, but I have to admit that I didn't quite understand it, let alone tried it."

"Visualization is a wonderful tool. You simply close your eyes and imagine what you want to come true. You're fantasising, Chiara! And you know how to fantasise. We all know that and we all fantasised, when we were children. And then we grew up. Never grow up to the extent that you stop fantasising, dreaming about the life you want. Because imagination is magical. And it's magical because it brings you a feeling that always precedes the manifestation you want to witness."

"I don't quite understand you."

"You know what people say: I'll believe it when I see it. Well, the path is reversed. First you believe, then you see. This life of ours is much more than what we've been taught. We're the creators of our lives, Chiara. Everything we believe, what we focus on and everything we think – we witness that in our lives. And why is this so? Because we live in a vibrational universe where there is one wonderful law, the law of attraction. And it is infallible. It simply gives you reflections of your vibration. It is like a mirror. It shows you what your thoughts are and what your focus is on. If you are positive, believe in yourself and life, believe that you can do something, that you deserve something, life gives you confirmation of that. If you are negative, angry at the whole world, think that life is unfair, then you get that back. Do you understand? You just get back who you are. Without any punishment or judgment of who should get what from life. You only get your own reflection. And when you understand that, you work on making your reflection beautiful. And you work on that in such manner that you become what you want to get back."

"Is that why everything is going so well for you?"

"Yes, my dear! I live this and that's why I know for sure that this works! And how it works! Also, I know I shouldn't have told you about this until you were ready. Yes, when people are ready to take their lives into their own hands and when they are tired of fighting life, only then are they ready to change. And that's a huge change in life, because instead of being a victim and

23

believing that life happens to them, they take life into their own hands and start creating it the way they want. Now let me show you how you can start changing how you feel right away. How do you feel when you say those sentences that you will never succeed, that Liam will leave you, that you will be alone in your old age?"

"Terrible!"

"Of course, because it is truly terrible. And now listen to these sentences: You live a wonderful love, Chiara. You have a husband who adores you. You have the kind of love in your life that many women may only dream about. You will become a mother. And at the best time, my dear. When you have your baby, you'll know exactly why it didn't happen earlier. The baby will come at the best time for you. You will love and adore your baby. You will live your dream, Chiara. You will! I am sure! How do you feel now, while listening to these words?"

"Great! It is the fulfilment of all my wishes."

"That's right. And nothing has changed around you this moment. You see, this is how we manage our emotions. We choose what we shall be telling to ourselves. We choose what thoughts we shall have. Because the way we feel shows the way we vibrate. And how we vibrate, that's what we get! We choose how we're going to feel. That is the difference that can distinguish you from the people that I told you about a moment ago. What we tell ourselves either gives us strength or robs us of that same strength. No one can tell you how to think. Then it's smarter to choose thoughts that will strengthen us!"

"But how can I think positive when everything is negative?"

"Honey, not all is negative! It's only negative when you get out of the present moment. All these words of yours from a while ago are negative and, because of them, you think that everything is negative. No situation in life has an omen, except the one we give it. If we see an event as negative, then it becomes negative. If we see it as a positive one, we witness a positive outcome. And you've heard of the saying: Our Thoughts Determine Our Lives. You tried it your way. Come on, try it in another one now! If the way you live doesn't give you the results you want, you need to change it."

"But how can I change my way, when the one I'm following now is the only one? It doesn't give results either. You know how much I tried to get pregnant naturally and nothing! They told us it was impossible and that we would never succeed like that. And we all know that even artificial insemination is not safe. What am I supposed to change, when I have nothing to change?"

"That is not to be changed. The way of thinking is to be changed. Let's try this: Do you know at least one person who was told that she would never get pregnant naturally, and yet she did?"

"I know, and you know her, too. Mia!"

"I know we both know her. That's why I am mentioning her. How is it impossible then, when there are people who were told it was impossible and they still succeeded?"

"But she first had a child through artificial insemination and then unexpectedly became pregnant naturally."

"That is exactly the point, my dear, sweet Chiara! When she stopped believing it was impossible, she witnessed it. Or to be more precise, when she let go of all the resistance keeping her in belief that she would never be able to conceive naturally."

"I'm afraid I don't quite understand you again", said Chiara, but now with a look that yearned for additional clarification.

"Mia had a child through artificial insemination. She became a mother. She was overjoyed. Every cell in her body vibrated with motherhood. She herself vibrated with motherhood. She made love with her husband completely relaxed, unlike all previous years. And she completely let go of the thoughts about having a child. She was no longer in need. And since the desire to have a child naturally was deep within her, the Universe 'delivered' a child to her. This is what creating reality looks like. When you achieve the vibration of your desire, it must manifest in your reality. It must! I didn't make this up. This is called the Law of the Universe that wiser people than me have been talking about for centuries."

"Okay, I get it now, but it was easy for her to vibrate, as you say, with motherhood. She had a child in her arms. What should I do? I don't have a child."

"There are more options, but I think the best for you are the two I'm going to suggest", Andrea continued, overjoyed that Chiara had taken an interest in a topic that could change her life.

"The first option is visualization. The second is dismissal, letting go.

Visualization is imagination. You close your eyes and imagine yourself with a child in your arms. You can imagine that you are pregnant, how you feel when the test shows positive result. You are free to imagine everything that will bring you a wonderful feeling. Through visualization, we achieve the feeling as if we were witnessing what we want. And we are starting to feel that way. And you know what is the most fascinating thing of all?! You start to vibrate like that. With your whole being, you send out the frequencies of what you imagine. And the Universe, in which the law of attraction works, has no idea that you are imagining it, and it doesn't even care. It simply gives you reflections of your vibration. That mirror I told you about a moment ago... These are called manifestations. When you tangibly witness in your physical reality what you once imagined and desired."

"Okay. And the other way?"

"The other way is even a faster way of creation, but unfortunately more difficult for most people. And that is dismissal. Realizing that you don't need what you want."

"What do you mean? I don't need it? So, if I want it, then I need it!"

"You don't need it, Chiara. You just think you do."

"Then why would I want it, if I don't need it?!"

"Everything you want, you want it because you think you'll be happy when you have it."

"Of course, I will be happy if I have something I want. I will be the happiest woman in the world when I get pregnant. I'm not happy now because I'm not pregnant. Pregnancy equals happiness. It makes sense to me."

"Logical and correct are not exactly the same thing. Prepare now for a little shock. Ready?"

"I don't know..."

"You don't really want to get pregnant. You want to be happy!" Andrea was greeted by silence. Chiara was looking straight into Andrea's eyes, processing what she had just heard.

"What are you saying?! I'm afraid you've lost me now. Please explain it to me."

"Yes, you want a child, that's a fact. But why do you want a child?"

"I want to become someone's mum."

"Why?"

"Because I want to be a mother! I want to have a child!"

"Yes, but why?"

"Because I want a real family. I want Liam and me to have a child we shall love and raise and enjoy our time spent together as a family."

"Yes, Chiara, I got you. But, why?"

"Well, because I want that! Because that's how I see our future. Because then I'll feel accomplished and happy!"

"Aha! There you go! What have we come to?"

"What do you mean?"

"What was the last thing you said? How will you feel?"

"Accomplished and happy", Chiara repeated her words, with her voice a little lower than before.

"Exactly, my dear friend. We have come to the emotion. And if for everything you want, you ask yourself why you want it, you will always get an emotion. And that's how you realize that everything we want in life is never about material things, business success, other people, but always about our desire to be happy."

"Okay. And what about that now?"

"This realization is the most important in life, because it completely changes your perception of life and frees you from all your needs. When you realize that you want everything because you think you will be happy then, you become wise and take a shortcut. You simply become happy! And you know what happens then?"

"What?"

"The magic of life, Chiara! Everything you want comes into

your life.

People who think they need something to be happy vibrate with a lack of having. They vibrate with the lack. That's why they don't witness what they want. They have no idea what they are doing. The more you want something, the more you vibrate that you don't have it. Because if you had it, the desire wouldn't be so strong. When you let go of desire and realize that you can be happy right now, you begin to vibrate with abundance. And the one who vibrates with abundance gets even more abundance. But as I said, only a few among us understand and achieve this. Because they need to learn to focus on the abundance they already live. And people have learned to focus on what they don't have, instead of the blessings they already have. The great news is that visualization is the way to dismissal, letting go."

"I don't know how much of this I understood, but thank you for all these explanations. Tell me, what would you do now, if you were me?"

"I would start with daily visualizations."

"Will you teach me to do that?", Chiara asked Andrea, grabbing her hand.

"Of course! Come! Let's go inside, to make you more comfortable."

They sat down in the living room. Chiara sat down in a comfortable armchair, and Andrea sat on the stool opposite her, just to be close to her.

"Come on, relax! Close your eyes and relax completely. Release the tension. Completely relax your body. I will help you. Just listen to me and do what I say. First, breathe deeply. Slow and deep. Let your inhale last as long as possible, as well as the exhale. You are not in a hurry. Focus on your breath. Feel the flow of air through your nostrils as you inhale and exhale."

Chiara did everything exactly as Andrea told her. She felt herself relaxing. She has always liked the moments when her brain is at rest and she doesn't feel the stress of her own thoughts and fears. With each inhale and exhale, she felt peace slowly permeating her body.

"Now we're going to relax your body. Focus on your feet. Relay them. Just consciously relax them. Feel all the tension leaving your feet. Now feel that relaxing sensation going up towards the joints and calves. You are completely relaxing the lower part of your legs. Then, the knees... Your lower legs are relaxing. Front and back. And now you feel the relaxation of your buttock and hips. Feel your whole legs relaxing even more, together with your buttock. Now take a few breaths in and out with your hips. And watch your entire lower body relaxing even more. Do that for two minutes."

Chiara felt this relaxation. What she was doing made sense. She felt a kind of peace and lightness that suited her.

"Now we shall do the same with the hands", continued Andrea. "Focus on your palms. Relax your palms, fingers and wrists. Feel them relaxing... Slowly relax your forearms, elbows and upper arms. Enjoy the feeling of relaxing your hands. Now, focus on your stomach and chest. Relax them. Although you breathe, breathing takes place in the rhythm of the relaxation and contraction of your muscles. Feel how wonderful it is to breathe completely relaxed. Now relax your back, your spine. Focus on your lower back. Give them a break. And slowly upwards, relax the whole back. Feel vertebra by vertebra. Feel the lightness and relaxation rising to your shoulders. And now let's relax the most important part of our body, the shoulders. Relax your shoulders. Take a deep breath... Keep going... Now exhale... Great job... Keep relaxing your shoulders. Let them fall down..."

Chiara enjoyed this part the most. With each exhale, her shoulders dropped a few inches lower. Only now did she realize how much tension she had in her body. Well, her shoulders were tense and raised all the time.

"Way to go, my dear! Relax your shoulders. Relax your shoulders. You don't need anything in them. Let it all come out. Observe how your whole body relaxes even more, as you're relaxing your shoulders".

Andrea was absolutely right. Chiara had the feeling that she was starting to float. She enjoyed this feeling.

"Now relax your neck. Feel your entire neck and head relaxing.

Your lips, jaw, cheeks, forehead relax... And relax your eyes. Completely relax the eye muscles. Feel how pleasantly they fall into your eyeballs and how your eye muscles are relaxed... I will leave you in silence for a few minutes, and you just keep your focus on your breathing. And if any thought comes to you, that's okay. It's natural. Don't fight them, you're not doing anything wrong."

The thoughts raced through Chiara's head. Not one, but many of them.

Every now and then she would remember yesterday and the negative test. She also remembered how excited they were the last time, thinking that they would succeed precisely that time. And then she remembered the moment of disappointment, when the test came back negative. She remembered her tears...

Andrea broke the silence: "If you're lost in your thoughts, just bring your focus back to your nose. To your breath. Keep bringing your focus back to the airflow."

Chiara was regaining her focus, but after a few seconds, the thoughts would start flooding in again. As if they were stronger and more powerful than her.

As if she knew what was going on in Chiara's head, Andrea, in a voice full of support, told her: "Give yourself time, honey. This is an exercise. I know it's not easy in the beginning to calm a mind used to work 24 hours a day, but don't give up. A calm mind is something that can be practised. And the more you practice, the longer the period of absence of thoughts shall be. Just don't fight it. Accept it as a process. Trust me, it's worth every minute invested. Let's do the visualization now. You will see its magic. Can you imagine yourself lying in your bed? A beautiful morning dawned. The sun is making its way through your curtains. That wonderful scent of morning. Can you see that image with your inner eye?"

"Yes, I can", answered Chiara, almost silently, because her lips were also completely relaxed.

"Excellent! Don't say anything more, just imagine what you hear. You wake up on that beautiful spring morning, you hear the chirping of the birds. Liam is next to you and you rush into his arms, bathed in the rays of the sun."

Andrea was just observing her. She saw her lips slightly stretch into a smile. A small smile, but still enough to see that Chiara is beginning to experience the image she sees.

"Observe how you feel. You're happy. You wake up in your beautiful house, next to a man whose love for you is endless."

Chiara felt warmth all over her body. She saw exactly how she was rushing into Liam's hug. He was holding her firmly in his strong arms. She felt him lowering her head on his strong chest, as if telling her with a tight hug: "Come, you are safe here".

"Live those feelings, Chiara. Live them! Don't take them for granted. Your awakening, right there, next to your husband, is something many women can only dream about. You're living it. It's real. Feel the gratitude for the love you live every day."

With her inner eye, Chiara saw, even more clearly, how she was hugging Liam. She could feel the blessing of that moment which, she had to admit to herself, she had been taking for granted in recent months. But now she brought it to her senses. And she decided not to do that, at least not for these few minutes, but to emotionally surrender completely to the love of a man who was pure love and support for her at all times.

"This morning you are in your perfect world, in your fairy tale you want to live. Now you realize that the two of you are no longer alone. You hear the light patter of feet entering your room. You hear the bedroom door open and your child runs towards your bed. And you hear: "Mum"!

Become aware of this moment in which you are a mum! Realize that your child slept in the room next to yours and it now comes to your bed, to cuddle with you. Feel free to choose whether you see a boy or a girl. Imagine whatever you want to imagine this moment..."

Her smile spread from ear to ear at these words. She started breathing faster and Andrea could clearly see the excitement vibrating out of her.

Chiara saw a beautiful blonde girl of four or five years of age, running happily towards them. She climbs onto their bed, throws herself into their arms and says: "Good morning, Mummy! Good morning, Daddy..."

The tears were pouring down her cheeks, but she did not open her eyes. In her thoughts, she was cuddling with her little daughter, daughter she wanted so fervently. She was a beautiful and indescribably sweet little girl. She crawled into the bed between the two of them, facing Chiara. Chiara looked at those beautiful little eyes, kissing her forehead, her nose, then kissing her forehead again and so on and on, while the little girl was laughing out loud the whole time, while visibly enjoying.

"Feel those emotions, Chiara. Feel them, live them", Andrea continued, knowing that at that moment she should not talk much, but let Chiara live these images, as clearly and as long as possible."

And Chiara has truly felt the most beautiful emotions ever. She felt an indescribable love for this sweet little girl whom she adored. She felt fulfilled and accomplished. She felt true joy and happiness after a long time.

"Now continue observing your day, Chiara. What does your morning look like? What are you doing together during the day? Are the three of you going somewhere together? Are you playing? How is your evening? Imagine whatever you want. Stay in it for a while. Don't worry about me. I have to go now anyway, and you just enjoy this experience. See you later."

Chiara heard her, but no answer came from her. Not only did she know she didn't have to, but she didn't want to interrupt this fairy tale she was witnessing.

Andrea silently got up from the stool and headed for the door, feeling indescribable joy for her friend who has felt the magic of visualization for the first time. Before she closed the door behind her, she, once again, directed her gaze at her friend who, with a smile from ear to ear, was sitting quietly in the armchair, clearly enjoying the scenes she was observing with her eyes closed.

When she opened her eyes, she realized she didn't know how much time had passed. And that didn't even matter. She felt wonderful. She was in the most beautiful story anyone had ever told, a story where Liam, their little girl, and her were a family. A story in which the three of them spent an unforgettable day, absorbing every moment spent together. For the first time, after a long time, she felt hope. Hope that this kind of life is possible. She reached for her cell phone and called Andrea.

"Welcome back", she heard the cheerful voice of her friend.

"Hi, my dear! Here I am! It was wonderful, Andrea!"

"I believe you, sweetie! That's the beauty of visualization. It helps you feel the emotions you will feel when you witness it."

"Uh, what emotions I had. And I realized I want a girl. She was beautiful, Andrea. Beautiful!"

"I believe she was. And she will be."

"She had beautiful blonde hair, the most beautiful eyes in the world, a small nose, and the most beautiful scent I have ever inhaled in my life. We cuddled for a long time. Then we prepared breakfast together, went to the park, went down the slide together, swung in the swing, played hide and seek. I lived through it all, Andrea! The best feeling in the world!"

"That's the most important thing, Chiara! The emotions you felt. They are essential in creation. Remember what I told you. What you emit is what you receive. The universe was listening to you. And the more often you have such emotions, the closer you are to actually witnessing it."

"And what now, when I don't imagine, but go back to the moments when it didn't come true?"

"Then you believe, Chiara! You believe we are able to create everything we want in life. When logic tells you it is impossible, let the voice of faith, telling you it is possible, be louder. I understand that people think imagination is fake and what we witness is true, but what you witness doesn't have to be permanent. But people believe it is, and it stays that way forever. The point of the visualization, apart from the fact that you sent a message to the Universe about what you want to live and what it should "deliver" to you, is to understand the most important thing I told you. Tell me, what was the most beautiful thing of all, while you were imagining it ?"

"Well, how happy I was", answered Chiara, without thinking.

"Exactly. Now remember what I told you this morning, but you didn't quite agree with me."

"That everything we want, we want it because of how it will make us feel when we have it."

"The happiness you felt was the point of everything. And you felt happiness by just imagining your child, right?"

"Yes, I understand it a little bit better now."

"When we do visualization, we slowly realize that the emotion we feel is the most beautiful part of it. And then, over time, we realize that we have come to this emotion by imagining. You weren't hugging your child in bed at that moment and you weren't really there, but you certainly felt happiness. You know, we have a choice at every moment of the day. Whether we shall worry or fantasize about what we want? We often get out of the present moment, but what makes the difference between people is the place to which they go. Many go into doubts, fears and worries. I go to faith, hope and optimism. I wasn't born under a lucky star and nothing has happened to me by chance. I've been doing this for a long time. I simply believed. Everything I imagine is like standing in front of a full buffet table and telling the Universe what I want to 'eat', if you understand me."

Chiara listened to Andrea very carefully. Maybe even for the first time.

Andrea already mentioned the sentence that we are able to create our own life, but Ciara had never heard it as clearly as now.

"Okay, I understand now. When I feel doubt, I just close my eyes and imagine the scenario I want. Right?", Chiara wanted to get the answer from Andrea.

"Something like that. If you just go with it, you have made a big change, not only in the way you think, but also in your vibration. The more you emit the vibration of motherhood, the closer you are to witnessing it. You know what's the best of all? You've got something to lose?"

"No. You're right. I am aware that the time for a change has come. Thank you, Andrea. Thank you for your friendship, patience and support from the first day we met."

"You're welcome, my friend! Believe me, my happiness has no end because I know how much this knowledge will change your life."

The following days were fantastic for Chiara. She felt great. The first thing she did was to take a rest. She listened to her friend who told her that it was perfectly fine to stop and simply recharge the batteries. She took time to discover herself and how she felt.

She bought a book on the power of the human mind and studied it in details. Every day she visualized and saw the future she wanted. She felt like she could fly from the energy she would feel afterwards. Liam and her didn't mention artificial insemination or new appointments. She decided not to worry about it for a while, but to simply enjoy it. Those were really beautiful days.

Tonight, Liam and her are going to dinner with Andrea and her husband. Andrea was on the trip and they hadn't seen each other for more than three weeks, and they both couldn't wait to meet again.

When they entered the restaurant, Andrea and Noah were already sitting at the table.

"Vow!", Andrea exclaimed. "Hi, Gorgeous! Where are you going tonight?", Andrea laughed when she saw Chiara.

"With you, ma'am", Chiara replied with a smile.

"You look beautiful, my dear!", Andrea told her, hugging her and kissing her on the cheek.

"Thank you, my dear! That's how I feel!"

"This lady of yours is getting younger and younger," Andrea addressed Liam.

"You're doing something right!"

"It seems so to me, too. But I wouldn't really take all the credits, there's definitely your influence in it", Liam replied to her with satisfaction.

"She has the most influence on herself. We are just watering her. Right, honey?"

"We are a dream team!", Chiara said happily, while sitting down at the table.

The evening went great. They talked about anything and everything.

They always liked to go to dinners together because they got along fantastically as a couple. They had a lot of common topics and always had a crazy time together.

At the end of the evening, when Liam and Noah retired to smoke cigars in the saloon, Chiara grabbed Andrea by both hands and spoke to her all excited:

"Andrea, you were right. This visualization of yours is truly a life changer! I don't remember when I felt as good as I have in the past few weeks."

"I believe you, my dear! I attribute the life I live to all these knowledge. I'm so glad you were open to it and saw how useful it is."

"Do you know what conclusion I have come to?", Chiara got all serious.

"I'm all ears," answered Andrea with a smile.

"I understood the most important things from what you told me. That I don't need anything from the outside world for happiness. As the days go by and I focus more and more on what I like in my life and I don't leave the present moment, unless I go in my imagination where I like, I feel better and better. I even had a moment of enlightenment, as some would say, where I realized that we are able to achieve a fantastic feeling, without anything around us changing in the reality!"

"Great job! That's it! That's what I told you about. Visualization leads you to that enlightenment, doesn't it?!"

"It does. You were totally right about everything. I owe it to you I feel this good."

"Not to me, honey! To yourself! You have achieved all of this. I just told you what I know and what I suggest. All my knowledge would be in vain if you didn't believe in it and start implementing it."

"Thank you once again for everything. It is a blessing to have you as a friend."

Andrea hugged Chiara with all her strength and let out a deep breath of relief, knowing that the best was yet to come for Chiara.

At that moment, Liam and Noah came back and it was time to go home.

They hugged and kissed, promising to repeat this kind of gathering very soon.

That evening, Chiara and Liam made love like they hadn't in months. She was kissing him consciously, not wanting to miss a single moment of his vicinity. She doesn't remember ever looking into his eyes like she did that night. She was looking into his eyes, actually looking into his soul. She was kissing not only his lips, but all the moments she spent with him. For the first time, she realized how absent she had been in their relationship and unaware of the moment in which she was living.

In recent years, making love for her has been the task that should have resulted in her getting pregnant. It was a pure duty, obligation. She didn't even enjoy it anymore, all because of the negative tests. And this wonderful man continued to show her only tenderness, love and attention. She was momentarily ashamed of this realization, but the very next moment she changed her mind, realizing that the feeling of guilt was of no use to her.

She was overwhelmed with a feeling of immense gratitude at the realization of how rich the woman already is and how she has a blessing that many women may only dream of. A wonderful husband who adores her and who always provided her with unconditional love, support and understanding.

Chiara, after a long time, felt happiness these days. That real, primordial and deep happiness because of the life she lived.

"I love you, Liam", she whispered softly, lying in his arms.

"Thank you for the love I feel from you. Thank you for all the patience you have had for me all these years. Thank you for never giving me criticism, judgement, or anything that made me feel bad. Thank you for being my unconditional support at all times. And forgive me, please, for my moments of weakness and moments when I lost focus on this blessing we live. I'm sorry that I was selfish and thought only of myself, forgetting that you also want a child, that you also want to be a dad, and no one was there to comfort you."

"Chiara, my love", Liam whispered softly, holding her even tighter.

"I have nothing to forgive you, honey. I understand everything, both now and before. I know how much it means to you to become a mum."

"But I forgot how important you are to me. How important this love we live is to me. And that's what I finally realized these last days. How much my focus was on what I don't have, while I completely forgot about all that I have. And I wouldn't trade you for anything in this world. I was ungrateful, Liam.

That's why I was unhappy. If something were to happen to you, I don't know how I would live without you. And I completely forgot that. I already have everything I need for happiness. I have love, your love, our love! And if I never become a mother, I know I can be happy. Because I'm already happy now! Happiness is not out there. It is here and now. We just don't see it running after something far away and seemingly unattainable. I already have everything!"

Liam wasn't interrupting her. He just let her talk, as always, knowing exactly the moment when not a word should be said. He was just stroking her hair gently, giving her a sign that he was listening to her.

Chiara was suddenly jolted out of her sleep by a flash of white light covering the entire ceiling of the room. She had to cover her eyes with her hands to protect them from the light. She looked at Liam who was sleeping next to her. They must have fallen asleep without even noticing.

"Liam! Liam!", she tried to wake him up, but Liam was fast asleep.

She turned her gaze back to the light. Now she could

already see it more clearly as her eyes adjusted to the intensity of the light. The whole ceiling looked like heaven. It was a beautiful light blue colour, bathed in white clouds. She had the feeling that the room had completely disappeared and that she was lying in a meadow, staring at the sky. She did not feel fear, but an indescribable peace.

As she was adjusting her gaze to the light, she realized that there were children sitting on the clouds. There were dozens of them. Now she could already hear the murmur of the children and their laughter.

Her body tingled from the wonderful moment she witnessed. The children did not look at her, but at a distance; as if they saw something she didn't. She wished she could hear them better. Floating, as if she came very close to them. They did not see her, at least they did not show that they have noticed her presence.

Her gaze stopped on a beautiful blonde girl, towards whom she felt a strong bond. The girl was sharing a bubble with an adorable boy, with whom she was talking about something. Chiara came completely close to them to hear them.

"When will you go to Earth?", the girl asked the boy curiously.

"I don't know yet", answered the boy, not sure in his words. "I'm still looking for my mum. And you? Are you leaving?"

"Yes. I'm finally leaving today! Great! You see, that's my mum now!", the little girl pointed her finger down and at the same time both the boy and Chiara looked down, following the little girl's finger.

Chiara lost her breath. The little girl was pointing towards the bed where Liam and her were sleeping. Chiara clearly saw herself sleeping in Liam's arms.

The tears were pouring down her cheeks uncontrollably and she was still in complete shock from what she had just witnessed.

"I chose her. A long time ago", the little girl continued in a cheerful tone.

"But she wasn't ready for me before", the little one kept talking. "She said that I would be her only meaning in life. That it would be the only important role in her life. That she would submit her whole life to me. And I didn't want that. I was waiting for her to understand that the beauty and meaning of life should be found without a child, that motherhood is one of the roles, but not the only one. That it is important, but not the most important! To understand that happiness comes from us, and not towards us. Because that's the only way we can share it with the others. And to learn to be happy with what she has. I was waiting for her to become grateful. If my life on Earth had started earlier, it would have been completely different than it will be now. Her happiness would depend on me and it would be too much of a burden for me. And now she is ready. Ready to be a wonderful mother and I will be able to live the life I want, with her support and guidance. Yes, I'm leaving now. I'm leaving to spend my life with the best mum in the world!"

Chiara was choking on tears. She fell to her knees, covering her face with her hands. It was like she was broken, but she didn't feel broken. She felt relieved. It was as if all the burden, which she had been carrying for years, finally fell off her shoulders. And these weren't the tears of sadness. She felt those tears rinsing her soul and all that she had been through. It was as if she saw life more clearly with each tear. She doesn't even know how long she stood like that.

When she calmed down, she removed her hands from her face and realized that she was back in her bed, next to Liam. The room was just a room again. The light disappeared; it was completely dark. She was completely confused, trying to figure out if it was all just a dream. She could feel her face, wet with tears. And her body was still trembling.

But she felt peace. It didn't even matter if it was all just a dream or not. The emotions she felt were real. She felt a change in herself, that she was no longer that old Chiara.

She let out a deep breath, clinging even tighter to Liam's warm body, drifting off to sleep, not knowing that very soon she would witness the greatest miracle of all. Two lines on the pregnancy test, which will confirm to her that this was not a dream. She really saw this little soul that chose her and Liam as her parents. The soul that was waiting to come as the result of the love between a man and a woman who, by living love and gratitude, will guide her through this magic called life.

Lilly & Rose

Rita was sleeping peacefully, until she heard a loud ringing. It took her a few moments to realize it was a sound of a phone. She looked at the clock – 3:35 AM. At the same moment, restlessness took over her whole body. All her life, she was afraid of that greatest parental fear – that the phone would ring at hours, when such a call could mean nothing good.

"Hello," she said in a frightened voice.

"Ms. Rita Martin?", a male voice was heard on the other side.

"Yes, this is Rita Martin."

"Are you the mother of Lilly Harris and Rose Walker?"

"Yes. These are my daughters. Did something happen to them?", she asked in a trembling voice.

"Mrs. Rita, I'm calling in the police name. Your daughters participated in a traffic accident this morning at 02:00. Both of them are located in the hospital of St. Helen, where they were urgently taken in serious condition."

She no longer heard the policeman. Her hand was shaking so much that she could no longer hold the phone still. Her legs gave out and she could barely stand. She began to cry uncontrollably, trying to catch her breath.

"What happened, tell me what happened?" Now, already shouting, Mrs. Rita manages to say through her tears.

"A truck driver, overtaking from the opposite direction, did not see them due to bad weather and collided head-on with their car."

"Are they alive?", Rita asked him, clinging to the wall with her last efforts, not to lose the ground under her feet.

"I don't know what's going on right now, but both of them still had a pulse when they were taken away. I suggest you go to the hospital and you will get all the information there. Both husbands were also informed. I'm sorry, ma'am. I will pray for you and your daughters", said the policeman, in a voice full of compassion.

Lilly opened her eyes, feeling an indescribable peace. She felt herself leaving her body, floating towards the ceiling of the hospital room. She saw everything clearly. She had a view of the entire room and the staff around her.

"We're losing her!", she heard the doctor. "Defibrillator urgently!"

There was a panic in the room, but she wasn't feeling that panic. She felt peace like never before in her life. She wasn't even confused by the realization that she saw her body on the operating table. She didn't even have a feeling that it was her. She was observing her body as a piece of clothing that she would take off when she got home. She knew it wasn't her. She was up here, free and peaceful, separated from the scramble and panic she was witnessing.

She could hear the thoughts of the nurses and doctors around her and feel their emotions, but she experienced it all as if she were watching a movie. She was able to feel them, at the same time not feeling that these emotions were hers.

In another part of the room, separated by a curtain, she saw the body of her sister Rose. She could see through the curtain. There were doctors and nurses around her and they were trying everything to keep her alive. Her body was blue and covered in blood, and some kind of wide transparent tube, connected to the machine next to her, was sticking out of her mouth.

Lilly felt no sadness. Exactly the opposite. She even wondered why all the panic, when she was feeling great. When she's not there anymore. She wished she could convey her peace to everyone present in the room.

"We are losing another sister, too! We can't lose them both! Can you hear me? We can't allow that!", she heard another doctor who was trying, with all his efforts, to bring Rose back to life.

A loud monotonous sound came from the machine measuring Rose's heart rate. Lilly could feel the panic in room again, although not a single word was spoken. "Lilly!", she heard a voice that gently addressed her.

She looked in the direction of the voice addressing her and next to her, on the ceiling of the room, she saw Rose. She was beautiful. More beautiful than ever before. Her skin was clean and white. Beautiful rays of light emanated from her and she radiated love.

"Hey, sis'! There you are!", Lilly exclaimed , feeling unconditional love.

She rushed into her arms and hugged her, as hard as she could. At that moment, they both felt love, peace and tranquillity at the same time. They loved each other endlessly throughout their lives. From the first moment they were together in their mother's belly and, as they liked to say, they were best friends, and not for 35 years, but for a year longer, because they began to feel mutual love in their mother's belly even before they took their first breath. Twins with an unbreakable bond from the first moment.

"What's going on, Lilly? Did we die?"

"Well, I don't feel like I'm dead", Lilly replied. "I feel more alive than ever."

"I think we died. I think this is what happens when you die", Rose replied , without any sadness in her voice.

Both felt the same. Calmness. As if they had nothing to do with the bodies lying on the hospital tables and the chaos that was happening around them.

"Come, let me show you something!", Lilly said, with determination in her voice.

It was as if she was the one who adapted to the whole situation faster.

In the next moment, as if in a flash, both found themselves on the ceiling of the hospital waiting room, where their husbands and mother were waiting for the news.

Their mother was sitting in an armchair, crying inconsolably. Lilly's husband, Adrian, was sitting next to her, holding her in his arms. He was staring at the wall, visibly worried. Rose's husband, Mario, was restlessly pacing the waiting room, talking on his cell phone. His eyes were filled with tears.

"Why are they so sad?", Rose asked.

"Because they think we're not well", Lilly answered her, in a voice full of tenderness.

"Hey, Mum!", Rose called out.

"We're here, Mum! We are fine! Adrian, Mario! "

"They can't hear you, Rose. They don't see us and they don't hear us."

At that moment, a huge flash of light appeared in the distance. As it was approaching them, both of them could see the silhouette of a person in the centre of that light approaching them.

As the silhouette came closer, they both began to feel an indescribable love. The love of that person for them who bathed them in the most beautiful emotions possible.

"Dad!", Rose exclaimed, recognizing him. "Lilly, it's Dad!"

At the same moment, they both found themselves next to him, merging into one embrace.

"Daddy, it's you!", Rose continued, vibrating happiness and excitement.

"How I missed you!", Rose said, not letting him go out of her hug.

"Daddy! I'm so happy to see you!", Lilly exclaimed happily,

hugging him as hard as she could. With that hug, she was trying to make up for the last seven years, during which she wanted to hug him so much. Their dad got sick nine years ago from lung cancer and died two years later.

"My dear girls!", the father said in a gentle and well-known voice they adored so much.

"Did you think I wouldn't meet you? So how can I not welcome my two favourite girls in the world?"

They were overjoyed to see him again. He looked fantastic. He looked exactly as they remembered him when he was healthy. He had the warmest eyes they had ever seen. He looked vital and healthy for a man of seventy years of age.

"Dad, you look exactly the same as you did before your illness!", Lilly addressed him.

"When we leave this world, we leave behind us everything we no longer need. We let go of our ego, all the limits of our mind, but also our body. Just like our diseases. We get sick due to all these limitations we carry with us while living a worldly life. At this very moment, you're seeing me as you remember me. Just like you're seeing yourselves at this moment. But, this is only to make it easier for you to adapt to this change. You'll soon realize that you don't need any of that here. That here you are the two souls, two beautiful bright lights, made of pure consciousness. This is how the beginning of the transition always looks like, so that the souls returning home are not too shocked, until they remember who they really are. They are always welcomed by their loved ones, who know how much comfort and joy these meetings will bring them."

"Dad, did we die?" Rose asked him. "At this moment, yes. But you can still choose to come back."

"Can we go back?", Lilly asked in surprise. "Yes. Every soul has a choice. That is our greatest gift from God. There is no soul that has returned home without being asked the question of whether it wants to continue life on Earth. There are the souls who make arrangements before leaving and already know for sure that they will not want to return to Earth, so they choose a way of transition, where it is impossible to return. But that was also their choice. And there are also a large number of souls who choose to go through the 'reminding school' of why they chose to go to Earth and whether their purpose was fulfilled. There is no wrong decision. There is not just one life. There is more than one life. Every soul knows that. And each soul decides for itself. All is always well. Whatever you decide. Come, I'm taking you somewhere."

At their father's words, a tunnel of light appeared above them and began to pull them upwards. They both felt themselves moving through the tunnel at incredible speed. At a speed they had never felt before. They didn't even know how much time had passed. As they travelled through the tunnel, they both felt as if time had stood still. More precisely, as if time didn't exist. Everything seemed to last a long time, and at the same time it seemed to happen in one second.

In what seemed like the next moment, the tunnel disappeared and all three of them found themselves above a beautiful meadow bathed in light, with the most beautiful flowers they had ever seen. The colours were beautiful.

All the colours they had known until then were twice as emphasized. Breath-taking beauty. The meadow was full of beautiful yellow butterflies flying carelessly through the air.

"Look at the butterflies!", Rose exclaimed with a smile. I love butterflies! My favourite creatures. Rose was excited. She adored butterflies all her life. While she was addressing her son, she used to call him: "My little butterfly".

Lilly's attention was drawn to three armchairs standing in the middle of the meadow, opposite a large screen that seemed to be floating in the air.

"Come, let's sit here!", their father invited them.

Dad sat in the middle, Lilly on his left, Rose on his right.

"It's time to remind yourself!", their father addressed them gently.

"Well, this is fantastic! It's like we're in the cinema!", Rose said through laughter.

"Like the good old days!"

"You are somewhat right", answered their father.

Lilly grabbed her dad's hand, not wanting to miss the moment that reminded her of her childhood.

"What are we going to watch, Dad?", Rose asked him.

"Your life. You will be able to see if you lived the life you wanted to live? You will be able to see how life really works and how you have affected other people's lives with your actions."

Before any of them bout could get their bearings, images of their lives began to appear on the screen.

They saw their birth. The joy of their mother and father when they realized they had twins. It was a surprise because, when their mum was pregnant, ultrasound did not exist yet, and their hearts beat as one, so even the doctor could not know that there were two babies inside. They were born a month too early and looked like two little buds. That's why they named them Lilly and Rose.

They saw themselves in incubators, fighting for their lives. What surprised them both was that they saw angels standing above their incubators in the hospital with their hands resting on them, filling them with strength and energy that strengthened them.

"Wow!", Rose exclaimed enthusiastically. "Angels!"

"Yes. They are always there with the children. Every child gets their own guardian angel when they come to Earth. For life. They were with you even today, when you had an accident. They are always there."

"But if they were with us, how come they didn't stop the truck from hitting us?", Lilly asked.

"Because it was your decision, a long time ago, to come back here at the age of thirty-five and remind yourself of all this. Each soul, before going to Earth, makes a decision about how long it wants to live a worldly life. When that time comes, they come back here to review their life and then make a decision whether they want to stay here or continue the journey called life."

"But most of them do not decide to return. Right, dad? And it was your decision not to come back, right?", Rose asked him, as if she already knew the answer.

"That's right! Most people, when they come back here and feel the freedom of this dimension again without the limitations of time and space, happily conclude that they want to stay here. Life on Earth is not easy. It takes a lot of inner work to live it consciously and happily, as our souls live here. There are few who we call Awakened and who reach a certain level of consciousness, enabling them to realize the freedom that their soul lives in every moment. These are people who truly live their lives! As well as those who decide to return with the knowledge they recall here. It is those who decide to return to life again, who return with a changed consciousness and never forget who they truly are and that there is no death. Then, for them, their mission changes and they become the ones who awaken others. I did not return because I realized my purpose was fulfilled. When I made a retrospection of my life, I realized that I had done everything I chose to do. Cancer was just an alarm with which my soul reminded me through my body that I was no longer enjoying life. You didn't need me like before. You have grown into two wonderful women, dedicated to your families and careers. I was ready to come back home."

"But you haven't met your grandchildren, Dad!", Rose said sadly.

"That's not really true", he answered her, pointing his finger at the screen.

Rose, at that moment, saw herself in the delivery room. Two years ago, on New Year's Day, she gave birth to her son. She was watching the scene she clearly remembers. The hospital suite where she gave birth, Mario standing next to her, holding her hand and giving her strength. She was moments away from giving birth. And then she saw something she hadn't seen then. Her father sitting on the armchair next to her, holding her baby in his arms. He cradled his grandson, looking into his eyes with a huge smile on his face.

"Dad! How is this possible?", Rose asked him excitedly.

"It's possible, sweetie. I held him before you saw him. And met him. I knew before you that you're gonna have a beautiful boy. All souls are here before they come to Earth. All of us who have left the Earth are with them before you. So, don't worry. I met your son and both of Lilly's girls."

Lilly melted at the thought. How many times she wished that her father had lived long enough to see her two little girls that she gave birth to three years after his death!

"That's wonderful, Dad! And how many people grieve when

their parents leave before welcoming their grandchildren!"

"Yes. They all realize that when they come here. That there was no need for sadness. Life is not exactly what it seems when we live it. If we know anything here, it's that everything is well..."

The screen starts showing their life again. They were watching their first steps, going to kindergarten, carefree games and moments spent with their parents.

They reached school days and a scene of Lilly appeared in front of them, when she was thirteen years old, entering school with her friends. At the door of the school, a boy approached her and shyly handed her a letter. It was a love letter. Lilly took the letter through a laughter and tore it up in front of the boy, continuing on, while all her friends were laughing derisively. Pieces of the letter were left on the floor next to the boy's feet. Lilly was watching the scene in shock.

"I don't remember this."

"Maybe you don't, but Toby remembers it. That's for sure. Now you will see how one of our actions can affect people and their whole lives."

Suddenly, a thirteen-year-old Toby appears on the screen, sitting in a room and writing a love letter to Lilly. Toby was very much in love with Lilly. For him, she was the most beautiful girl in the world. When he wrote the letter, he stood in front of the mirror encouraging himself: "You can do it, Toby! Give her a letter tomorrow. She needs to know how much you love her. You will not be embarrassed."

In the next scene, they saw Toby standing in tears, at the school doors. All the children were laughing at him. He cried on the way home. That event changed him. Lilly could see the whole course of his adult life as an insecure man who never regained his confidence because of that event at school. To this day, he remained alone, as a thirty-five-year-old man who drowns his sorrows in alcohol.

Lilly was silent. The tears were rolling down her cheeks. How could she be so rude and insensitive to that boy?!

"Did I really influence his whole life with one such action?"

"Yes!", her father answered.

"He has never recovered from that. He has never become aware that this particular event was the cause, but that moment, when he was embarrassed and ridiculed by the whole school, caused his further image of himself. All the choices and decisions he made in life, he made because of that low level of self-confidence, at which he remained. Don't feel guilty Lilly, you didn't know. You were just a little girl. It is not up to us to feel guilty for the decisions and choices of the others. Everyone has the free will to work on themselves and change their life, if they're not happy and life does not give them the results they want. All of us unknowingly hurt the others sometimes. Therefore, it is important to be as good a person as possible because you never know how much your harsh word or action can affect someone. Just like a nice word or gesture."

At those words of her father, Lilly appeared on the screen again, this time at the age of thirty, standing in line at the store. In front of her, there was a barefoot woman with a child at the cash register, paying for four cups of yoghurt.

"Four Euro," the cashier said.

"What do you mean, four Euro?", the woman asked the cashier.

"It said that these were on special sale. Four cups for two Euro."

"No, ma'am. These are not on special sale. You got that wrong."

"OK then, I'll just take two of them."

"I'll pay for you, ma'am!", Lilly said, handing all four cups of yoghurt to the woman.

"It's OK. I will pay, along with my stuff."

"Thank you, ma'am!", answered the woman, thanking her not only with words, but also with a look.

Lilly remembered this event. What she didn't know was what happened after that.

The screen showed a woman who had left the store, overjoyed that she had two Euro that she hadn't spent. After a few minutes, she decided to enter a kiosk selling the lottery tickets. She bought a scratching post for one Euro and won a cash prize in the amount of one hundred and fifty thousand

Euro!

Her life changed fundamentally. Her good deed started a chain reaction that she has never found about, until now. She saw her whole life after that, but also the life of her child. Everything looked completely different than it would have, if Lilly hadn't done it.

"This is wonderful!", Rose applauded.

"It really is!", Lilly confirmed, feeling a wonderful warmth around her heart.

"Every action we take affects other people. Each one. And we never get to find out how we influenced someone. But every person reviews their whole life when they come here and see whether they have had a positive or negative impact on other people's lives", continued the father.

They watched their whole life on the screen. They also saw other people's stories. They saw that Rose's manager, who insulted and mistreated all the other employees, including Rose, was actually a very unhappy person. She had a husband who was away from home for days. When he came, he would insult her, saying that she was a poor mother, that he could not eat what she cooked because it was not even close to the quality of his mother's cooking. She was seen countless times sitting and crying on the bathroom floor. And to what extent her behaviour at work was actually a call for help. They could clearly see that her rude attitude stemmed from her pain.

Rose felt love for her.

"God, I didn't know this. If I had, I would have treated her completely differently. Well, she needed a friend, and we all hated her and rolled over our eyes when we saw her. We never asked her out for drinks with us after work", Rose said in a sad voice, realizing how wrong she was.

"You couldn't have known that, Rose", her father told her.

"But now you clearly see how every person who attacks another person is crying out for help. Angry and aggressive people are full of pain. Such people need love the most. Every person who has inner restlessness manifests it outwardly. On other people. Because of the helplessness they feel. By this you can always recognize who is having the internal struggles. A happy person has only one need, and that is to share their happiness with the others."

As the father uttered those words, everything suddenly went dark, while a bright light appeared in the distance, heading towards them at incredible speed. It wasn't a person, but it seemed like it was. It was as if they knew the entity approaching them, and yet they didn't. They felt that they were in the dark and yet in the light. They have never experienced anything like that. It approached them and, without any words, said: "It's time for you to come with me!".

And before any of them both became aware of what was going on, the light pulled them inside. It was as if they let go of their bodies and merged with the light from that moment on. Each of them was simultaneously an orb, entity, consciousness,

intelligence, strength, power, love – all in one. They felt that
they were a part of it, and yet, as if they each had their own
individual consciousness for themselves at the same time. They
floated through the Universe through the stars in that shiny ball
of light, completely surrendering to the love and security they
were leaving. The light, in which they were, spilled over them
and in them. They became a part of it. They became knowledge
and pure consciousness. They both felt like they knew this place.
They recognized it. They felt freedom. They felt themselves
letting go of their old bodies, without any need for attachment.
They felt freedom. Freedom of pure consciousness, without
any need for anything. They were everything and they were
nothing. They were big and small. They were inside that sphere
and outside it at the same time. They could see everything
around and inside them. They were energy. Pure energy. At
that moment, they merged into one. They were no longer
two consciousnesses. They were one consciousness. And they
remembered. They remembered that they were like that before.
One soul, one consciousness. They recognized each other. They
came back to themselves. They returned home. Free from ego,
personality, character, mind, thought, pain, attachment, body.
There was no fear. Only peace, existence and love. Endless love,
and that's what they've always been.

The orb of light dissipated and they could see stars, millions
of them. Each one individually and all together at the same time.
A portal appeared in front of them, calling out to them, without
a word being spoken. They consciously headed towards it. They
saw the planet Earth and at the same time all the people on it.

Each individual on it. At that moment, a large white ball of light appeared over the planet and exploded into 8 billion orbs, with each orb going towards one person. The orbs entered the bodies of the people on the planet and illuminated their hearts. Every person on the planet was glowing. The sisters felt indescribable love in the knowledge of unity. They also became aware of the light in them. They felt a bond with every person on the planet. They could, once again, see their influence on every person they met in their lives. But this time they could also feel the emotions of those persons They were able to feel their joy or sadness. Now they felt the pain of every person they hurt along the way. Magnified a hundred times. They also felt every joy they caused. They did not feel that they were being judged. They didn't judge themselves either. They were just observing. But they felt absolutely everything.

They knew how loved they were at this moment. And, although they felt other people's pain, they also felt love at the same time. They bathed in an unconditional love, feeling that it was a part of them and they were a part of it.

Both of them heard a voice was telling them: "You are loved. You are infinitely loved. You have always been a part of Me and will always be. You have never been separated from Me. I have always been with you and in you. You couldn't do anything without Me feeling it too. No matter what was happening, the light in you was stronger. Love has always been in you."

At that moment, all the people on Earth lit up with a stronger intensity, but both of them could now clearly see the shadows on their eyes.

"Every person in the world" the light continued its speech, "carries love within them, but many people have shadows over their eyes preventing them from seeing who the others really are. It's not accidental. In order for people to know who they truly are, it is necessary to play this game of life in which they forget who they are and that they are all one, that they are all love. They look at each other, but they don't see each other. By living life, feeling and giving love, they remind themselves more and more who they are, and the shadows from their eyes disappear. Love and knowledge reveal to them who they really are. That's why some of them know who they are, and some don't. Nothing happens by chance. It's all a part of My plan. From the beginning to the end. Everything is as it should be. All is well."

"The time has come for you to decide if you want to return", the voice told them.

At that moment, they separated again into two orbs, with two different consciousnesses. Again, they had body silhouettes. They stood opposite each other, but did not see each other. They saw images of souls before coming to Earth and the arrangements they make. They saw a beautiful luminous ball from which two orbs, two souls, separated.

"The two of us are going to be sisters", they heard one soul saying these words.

"Let's live the experience of twin sisters this time. To see what it's like to be born and have a best friend at every moment of your life, but also to overcome the challenges of our own individuality. The environment will treat us all our lives as one person, so that we learn to keep each of our personalities, without the feeling of competition."

"I agree", another soul answered.

"Great mission. With the love and connection, we will feel, we will learn to see both ourselves and other people outside the box. Oneness that lives as duality. A wonderful mission."

At that moment, three more orbs came out of the great light from which their two souls came out.

"We shall come as your daughters!", shouted both souls in unison, addressing the soul that will be Lilly.

"And I will come as your son!", said the third soul, coming to the soul that will be Rose.

Lilly and Rose could now see all the arrangements they had made before coming to Earth. First they looked together at the arrangements Lilly had made with these little souls. They saw that Lilly chose, apart from her mission to show individuality with her life, to live life as a mother of two little girls. To be a role model of a woman who will manage to find a phenomenal balance between her business passion and parenthood. She will be the mother who will teach them the most by her example. Both girls will be leaders in their chosen professions in the ways, they observed their mother, and with their knowledge will influence a huge number of people to realize their dreams, but also to realize how strong and capable they are. Thus, Lilly could see how much her life, like a domino effect, would have an impact, not only on her daughters, but also on further generations of people, and even hundreds of years in advance. She saw that she would choose to return here, when her daughters were already mothers, with families of their own and successful careers. She will return here when her mission is complete.

Now they were looking at the arrangements Rose had made with the soul that would come as her son.

Both souls wanted to repeat the mission to help people in difficult moments of pain and loss of their loved ones. They saw that in the past experiences they had chosen before coming to Earth, the soul of Rose and the soul of her son had switched roles. Rose was a child then, and the soul that would be her son was her mother in a past experience.

In her past life, Rose was a child who left the world too early by earthly standards, and the soul that was then her mother dedicated her life to working with parents who lost their children too early, offering them, through the foundation and lectures, comfort about how our loved ones never truly leave, and her work made parents aware of how to live after the loss of a child. They also saw how many parents they helped. How many parents have they given a new perspective on life and taught them to continue living the life their children would want for them. It was a wonderful mission for both souls. That's why they wanted to repeat it, but this time they wanted to help children who lost their parents too soon. That's why they will switch roles this time. Rose will come as a mother and, by earthly standards, leave the world too soon.

Because of Rose's decision not to return to Earth, her son will grow up to be a wonderful man full of understanding for those who lose their parents too soon. They saw that he would write several books on the subject of death and that he would live his life in a way that would make Rose proud of him. Due to Rose's untimely departure, her son will increasingly remember who he really is and their agreement, and will provide people with insights into the choices of souls and the possibility that death does not exist as an end.

He will establish the Butterfly Souls foundation dedicated to his mother, who adored them.

They could clearly see the millions of people he would comfort and strengthen through this work.

The images disappeared and Lilly and Rose could see each other again. They looked at each other without a single spoken word, feeling endless love for each other, as well as for everything they had just witnessed.

"I think this is goodbye, Rose", Lilly said quietly, realizing that Rose would not choose to return to Earth.

"It's not, Lilly! This is not a final goodbye! This is not the end, but until we meet again", Rose said with a smile, rushing into her arms.

The sisters held each other tightly in their hug, feeling no sadness. Holding each other like that, they could feel that they were again one. That they have always been one and that they will remain one forever.

"I know you'll always be there for my son", Rose whispered softly to her ear, still holding her tightly. "Remind him every day how much I love him. Remind him that I will be with him all the time. Tell him everything. Remind him daily of who he is and that because of my endless love for him, I chose not to return. Tell him there won't be a moment I won't be by his side."

"I will Rose, I promise!", Lilly said.

"I will miss you!"

"I am here and I will always be here. There won't be a moment when I won't be by your side. And one more thing. When you see a little yellow butterfly, know it's me!", Rose said with a smile on her face, hugging her sister as hard as she could.

"See you, Rose!", Lilly said, feeling like she had to go.

"See you, sis'!", Rose answered, merging with the light again.

"And, Lilly, don't forget: All is well!!!"

Lilly slowly opened her eyes. The rays of the sun came through the window of the hospital room. She could hear the birds chirping through the open window. She turned her head towards the window, breathing in the scent of the spring morning. At that moment, she did not know how much time had passed since the accident. She would later find out that she had been clinically dead for nineteen minutes and had been brought back to life in a last effort.

The last two days were full of anxiety for her family, as they waited to see if she would wake up.

"She's awake!", she heard her husband's voice.

At the same moment, she saw her mother and husband standing over her bed.

"Lilly, honey, welcome back!", Mom said through tears of relief, caressing her cheeks at the same time.

"Thank you God, thank you!"

Her husband sat next to her on the bed, holding her hand.

"Lilly my love!"", he said with tears in his eyes, caressing her cheeks.

"How are you honey, how are you feeling?"

Lilly looked into his eyes, in complete peace and tranquillity, remembering everything she had seen and experienced.

At that moment, a small yellow butterfly flew in through the window of the hospital room, landing on the edge of Lilly's bed. Lilly noticed it. A smile spread across her whole face.

She looked at that beautiful yellow butterfly for a few

moments, feeling the presence and endless love of her sister.

She looked back at her husband, grabbing his hand and looking into his eyes, and quietly said:

"All is well......"

Leonard

Leonard was awakened by a bright light that was directed at him.

"Get up!", he heard a strict voice and felt someone kicking him with a foot.

"Get up and get out of here! This is not a dorm for bums!"

Because of the light, he could barely recognise the policeman standing above him.

"I have nowhere to go", Leo said.

"You should have thought about that earlier. You have two minutes to get out of here", said the policeman and headed towards the car.

Leo got up and started to fold the cardboard he had been sleeping on.

He stuffed the blanket he used to cover himself into a large backpack, which was all he had, looked at the policeman once more and started walking. He didn't know where to go now. It was two o'clock in the morning and the wind was blowing hard. That's why he stopped in the lee between two buildings, because that was the only place that would protect him from the cold at that moment. He knew that all the "good" places were already taken. He continued walking, until he saw a bridge under which he thought he could settle down for tonight. When he got under the bridge, the wind was still blowing heavily, but he had no choice. He barely spread his cardboards, fighting to keep them from being blown away by the wind. He used a backpack instead of a pillow and wrapped himself in a blanket. This was going to be another long and sleepless night, he thought.

Leo managed to fall asleep. Again, for the umpteenth time, he dreamed the worst day of his life. The day he found out that his business partners had deceived him and that his company was completely bankrupt. These were not only his business partners, but also friends. At least, that's what Leo thought. He trusted them completely and never had the slightest suspicion that they were working behind his back. Leo ended up on the street very quickly.

Completely alone. Without anything. The only way he currently survives is by begging on the street. There is no way out.

He thought that he will be spending the rest of his life like this.

When he woke up, he headed to the busiest street to beg for some money. When the traffic light turned red, he would knock on people's car windows, reaching out to give him a few cents or Euro to get him through the day. He experienced all kinds of things. From compassionate people who would help him without thinking to people who ignored him as if he didn't exist. There were also those who would insult him, call him derogatory names, even spit on him. He never got mad at them; he knew what they probably thought of him. That he is a low-life and an alcoholic who got here by his own decision. He knew they didn't know his life story. He got used to it all these six months, during which he was living on the street.

A large black Jeep with tinted windows stopped at the traffic light.

Leo couldn't see who was inside. He knocked on the passenger window anyway. At that moment, the window rolled down. Leo saw a very decent gentleman inside and was intoxicated by the scent of his perfume. He looked very rich.

Leo reached out to take the money, when instead of money, the gentleman put a book in his palm.

"My dear friend", the man addressed him.

"Now I will give you a much greater gift than the one you came for. What you think you want would help you get through the day, and what I'm giving you will help you to change your life. Don't miss this opportunity."

Leo was taken by surprise and couldn't get a word out.

The light turned green and the horn of the car behind sounded.

While the Jeep driver was moving slowly, he addressed him once more:

"Listen to me. I gave you the most valuable thing I could give you at this moment. Don't waste this gift."

Leo stepped back without a word, as the light turned green and the cars sped down the road again. Leo put the book in his backpack and continued to wait for the red light.

When the night fell, he went to the grocery store and bought himself a few cans of fish and beans and a pack of apple juice. Today he has to find a place to sleep early, not to spend the night in the wind again. He arrived before everyone else in the street, in which where sleeping was allowed . He got the best place today. He set up his cardboard and started eating his dinner. When he was taking cans out of his backpack, he noticed that book.

He took it out and looked at it, while he was having dinner.

Change your life in 30 days, he read to himself.

Yes, that's possible, as if!, he thought. But then he remembered the man who gave it to him. Why would that man do that? Why would he give him a book, instead of money, which he certainly had.

His words still echoed in his head:

"I gave you the most valuable thing I could give you at this moment. Don't waste this gift."

What have I got to lose?!, thought Leo. It's not like I have any responsibilities for the next thirty days, he thought and continued with his dinner.

When he was done with his dinner, he lay down on his cardboard bed and opened the first page of the book.

This is the most important book you will ever read; Leo began reading the preface.

Do you believe that in 30 days you can live a completely different life than the one you are living right now?

Well, not really, he said to himself, but I'm willing to try, he was honest. He couldn't stop thinking about the man who gave him the book. He was once that successful and knows what kind of mindset it takes for such a success. If such a man made the decision to give him a book instead of money, there must be a good reason for it.

There is no situation, he continued to read, **that you are currently in without a way out. And if you are at the absolute bottom, without any income and a roof over your head, all that can change in the next thirty days.**

Leo paused. He recognized himself in these words. Well, that's him. He's at the very bottom of life now.

In this book you will learn how to change your life in just thirty days. You will learn the secret that will lead you to your desired lifestyle. What is important is that you follow the instructions in the book and the methods I will recommend. Implementation is the key here. If you are currently unemployed, the great news is that you have all the time in the world to work on yourself and what you will learn here. I hope you are ready to change your life from the roots and start living the life you were created for and you deserve.

Ready? Let's go...

Leo turned to the next page. He was ready. So, he wanted to have a roof over his head again, to feel like a man. He hasn't felt like this for six months. He became invisible in society. He doesn't exist. He contributes nothing, does nothing to feel valuable, has no friends, no family. It is very difficult to feel like nobody and nothing. He wants to find a way out of this situation, but right now he's not able to find it himself.

First step on your way towards a change – it was written in the title.

What you are living this moment is what you believe is the way it should be. What you have experienced so far and what you are witnessing at this moment. But this truth is not cemented. You can change the truth. You are much more than that body you carry with you and that mind that is always looking for logical explanations. In order to change your life, you need to learn how to change the truth.

Many of us think that life is meant to be observed and that's how they live it, as observers. No, it's not like that! Life is meant for us to create it, and then to live our creation. I know that this is completely new for many of you who are reading this right now. But, try to hold on and read to the end, because soon everything will become much clearer. I will give you a task that will prove to you that you are able to bring into your life what you think and decide to bring into

your life.

Starting from tomorrow, you can change your truth that you are living right now. How?

So that you change your perception of life, start thinking thoughts that serve you and, most importantly, start feeling as if you were already living what you want right now.

Your vibration plays the biggest role in your life. Your vibration is how you feel. Your emotions are nothing but energy in motion. And when that energy is positive, more precisely, pleasant (hope, joy, faith, gratitude, optimism...), it is a sign that your vibration is also high. When your emotions are negative, more precisely, unpleasant (fear, envy, anger, pessimism...), it is a sign that your vibration is low. You can exactly tell how you vibrate by how you feel. This is the vibrational universe, which, like a mirror, sends us a reflection of our vibration. If you want to receive what you want, you must first learn to vibrate that way.

This is how you change your truth, and thus your life. First you change your vibration, then you start getting your own reflection. It is already happening to you. The only question is: Are you aware of it?

Leo paused in his reading and remembered the moment he found out he had been deceived. He was in the greatest fear he had ever been in. He hated the people who did this to him. He lived in hatred and anger from the moment he found out about the fraud. He even had a strong desire for revenge. And sank deeper and deeper. He doesn't remember the last time he felt a glimmer of hope that something could change. And now he lived in the belief that every day would only get worse.

The first step towards a change is changing your focus, he continued reading. **When we are in a difficult situation, we very easily fall into the trap of seeing only the bad things. The good things around us seem to no longer exist. The blessings that we have for us even at that moment become invisible.**

We have to change that first. When we start to change our life, we need to understand that we cannot magically change where we are now, but we can change how we feel. At least for a few minutes a day. Don't forget that. How we feel is what we emit.

The first exercise I want to share with you is the gratitude exercise. Gratitude is a spell that represents the first step towards your transformation.

For the next two days, every night before you go to bed and every morning when you wake up, be aware of the good things in your life. And count your blessings. You must have them. Right now, you must have something that no one else has. By focusing on whatever form of abundance you are experiencing right now, you begin to vibrate with abundance. Even if something seemed small and unimportant at that moment. It's not true! Don't take anything for granted. By focusing on at least one thing that works for you at that

moment, your focus will shift from lack to abundance. And you will feel a little better, at least for a moment. Just enough to shift your vibration.

Do not continue reading this book until those two days go by. I promise you that during those two days you will already experience some changes in your life and see for yourself how powerful this easy first step is to bring you something new and beautiful.

Leo closed the book. He didn't want to continue reading, he was going to do exactly as it was written.

What does he have to lose? Absolutely nothing. He wasn't really convinced by what he read, but he still couldn't get the man who gave him the book out of his head.

He made himself more comfortable in his cardboard bed and thought about what was good in his life right now.

I'm sleeping in a great place tonight, he thought. Yesterday I was in the wind and cold, today I'm not Yes, I can be grateful for that right now. I have a blanket to cover myself with, he continued. Someone is missing it and feels the coldness at this moment. Today I saved enough money and ate well. I'm not hungry, he continued counting thing for which he was grateful. I am grateful for that. Nothing hurts me. Regardless of the fact that I haven't seen a doctor in six months, my health is serving me, thank God. There, I can be grateful for those three things, he thought and continued talking to himself. Um, yes, how long has it been since I thought positively like this. It makes sense, he continued.

Leo fell asleep at that moment.

Leo was woken up by the sun. He doesn't even know what time it is because he doesn't have a watch. He opened his eyes, aware of how well he had slept. Almost every night he has nightmares about the past and how he ends up on the street again and again. That didn't happen last night. He slept peacefully.

As soon as he opened his eyes, he remembered the book. It's impossible that the task is the reason for my peaceful sleep, he thought. Must be a coincidence. Regardless of his scepticism, he decided to continue with the task. He sat up and stretched his arms. He leaned against the wall behind him and began to contemplate.

What a wonderful day, he thought. It wasn't cold. Well, today I can be grateful for this sun, he immediately realized that he saw it. He looked around, realizing that what his eyesight also be considered a blessing. He remembered Martin, whom he sees on the street and who is blind, and they go through the same negative stuff, except that Martin is blind. How much harder it must be for him!

Then I can be grateful that my eyesight serves me, he continued, proud of himself for even having that thought. I can be grateful that I am able to walk, he continued to list all his physical features, in which he is not limited. From three things he is grateful for, he has come to seven. Interesting, he said to himself when he finished.

Time to get to work, he said aloud, making himself laugh. At that moment he stopped. He heard his own laughter. My God, I laughed, he thought. How long had it been since he heard himself laugh.

He picked up his cardboard, put the blanket in his backpack and headed towards the street to 'earn' money for today's meal.

After an hour of begging, Leo barely managed to get enough money to buy himself a breakfast. He went into the bakery to buy a pastry and yoghurt. While he was waiting for his turn, he heard a little girl behind him saying:

"Mum, why is this man so dirty?" Leo didn't turn around.

"Honey, that man is homeless", the mother answered quietly.

"And what does that mean, mum?", the little girl continued

"That means he doesn't have a house to live in."

"What do you mean, he doesn't have a house?", the little girl continued, confused.

"No house, honey. He lives on the street."

"So where does he sleep?", the little girl continued with her questions.

"Well, everywhere, on a park bench, in some alley, I don't

know where, but he doesn't have a roof over his head."

"Mom, that's terrible!", continued the little girl.

"Yes, my love, it's sad", continued the mother sympathetically.

"Who knows what story this man has."

Leo was silent. He didn't want to turn around so they wouldn't realize he heard them. But it was nice not to feel judgement after a long time. Otherwise, people always judge him. They avoid him, show disgust, push him away. This mother and this little girl seemed to see him as he truly was.

When it was his turn, he told the saleswoman what he wanted to say and when he reached for the money in his pocket, he heard the mother's voice again:

"Sir, would you do me the pleasure and let my daughter and me treat you with a breakfast?"

Leo turned now. He saw a beautiful young woman next to him. Shoulder-length blonde hair, beautifully groomed, beautiful lips stretched into a wide smile. She smelled like the most beautiful flower.

He looked down at the little girl who looked just like her mother. She had long blonde hair with beautiful curls and two little butterflies in her hair that held her hair back so it wouldn't fall on her face.

She was dressed in a white coat and looked like a little angel.

The little girl looked at him with big brown eyes, a wide smile revealing her small white teeth.

Leo felt a warmth around his heart that he hadn't felt in a long time. He could hardly stop himself from bursting into tears. The emotions that overcame him at that moment of human kindness, as if, after a long time, took him by surprise.

"Thank you, ma'am!" Leo barely managed to say something.

"Thank you endlessly for your kindness."

"That's nothing, sir! It's the least we can do right now."

"Could you please give us two muffins and two cups of yoghurt?", she now addressed the saleswoman.

"And we'll also pay for the gentleman."

The saleswoman put two muffins, one pastry and three cups of yoghurt in the same bag, which she then handed over to the lady.

At that moment, Leo looked at the little girl. Her eyes were shining. She was looking at him with such tenderness that Leo couldn't help but smile back at her.

"There you go! Come with us, we will give you your things outside." They came out, in front of the bakery.

"Here, we will take our things out of the bag, so you keep it.

I have a spare bag in my purse," she said, opening the purse and taking out another bag.

"Thank you again, from the bottom of my heart," Leo said,

giving her a grateful look.

"You're welcome, sir. Here you go". said the woman, handing him the bag.

"And what is your name?", the little girl asked him. "I'm Leo", he answered.

"I'm Heidi", the little girl answered.

"And this is my mum. Her name is Zara."

"Nice to meet you", Leo said, while smiling.

"Nothing, we're going now, so that we don't keep you any longer", said Zara.

"Thank you once again from the bottom of my heart", Leo replied.

"Goodbye!", Heidi shouted, giving her mother a hand and walking towards the pedestrian crossing.

Leo stayed where he was and watched after them. Their backs were now turned to him. It was wonderful to see them like that. He saw that the little girl continued posing questions to her mum. They talked the whole time, while they were waiting for the green light to turn on. Leo turned and started walking back to where he was begging.

After a few seconds he hears a voice:

"Mister Leo, Mister Leo!", he heard a voice that was already familiar to him.

He turned and saw Zara and Heidi hurrying towards him.

"Excuse me, please, but Heidi had an idea. She would like to buy you new clothes and shoes. She says that she has her own savings and that she would be the happiest girl in the world to do that for you. Come with us to the next street. There is a store with used clothes and shoes, so let's go and get you what you need. Do you want to come with us?"

Heidi kept her eyes on Leo. She excitedly waited for Leo's answer with wide eyes and a wide smile, now well known to Leo.

"Well, that's a very nice present, sweetie!", replied Leo, not wanting his shame to overcome the joy and excitement of this beautiful girl. He definitely needed new clothes and shoes, so this was truly a blessing.

"Great! Let's go!", shouted Heidi, reaching to her mother again and the three of them headed towards the clothing store.

They left the store with three bags. Zara bought everything she thought Leo needed. Boxers and undershirts, two pairs of pants, two pullovers, a winter jacket, a pair of shoes and a new blanket.

"Now we've solved that, too", Zara said with a smile.

"Do you like the things we bought?", Heidi asked playfully.

"Yes, Heidi. Thank you for the gifts", Leo said, not forgetting how much it meant to the little girl that she was going to buy him this.

"Mr. Leo, just a little something before we go", Zara said, reaching into her purse and taking out her wallet.

"You've already done too much for me", Leo said, realizing what she wanted to do.

"It's not too much", Zara answered. "In fact, all of this is nothing."

She reaches into her wallet and hands him a 50 Euro note.

"That's too much, Mrs. Zara!"

"But really, it isn't. Heidi gave you clothes, and I want to give you this. Take it, please. It would mean a lot to me."

Although he would have preferred to refuse the money because he was already embarrassed, Leo held out his hand and accepted it. He knew how much 50 Euro meant to him.

"Thank you endlessly", he said.

"To you too, honey. You are two beautiful human beings."

Heidi smiled at him, in her now well-known smile.

"Good luck, Leo!", Zara told him. "Until next time!", she smiled gently at him and took Heidi's hand.

"Come on, Heidi, we're seriously late for your piano lesson now."

"Bye!", Heidi shouted to him, hopping along with her mother.

Leo felt wonderful. He had a new wardrobe, a new blanket and enough money for a few days. He felt rich. That thought made him laugh, too.

How little do we need to feel like we have a lot, he thought and went to find a place to rest.

He sat down in the park on a bench where homeless people were allowed to hang out. Homeless people were not allowed to sit everywhere in the park because they would be chased away. He sat down and thought about everything that had happened to him today. This day was really strange. A day like

he hasn't experienced in a long time. He felt that someone was seeing him again after a long time, that he was worth something. It was a very good feeling.

Today, after a long time, he will be able to go to the canteen and eat a hot meal. After that, he will find a place to change into new clothes, and he will leave these somewhere for the people who share his fate. He doesn't have to beg today. This was a good day.

When the sun went down, Leo managed to settle in the same place as yesterday. Again, he came among the first because he didn't have to beg late into the night. He adjusted his cardboard and took out a new blanket from his backpack. It was much warmer than the one he had so far. He saw the book in the backpack again.

Oh!, he said out loud, as if he remembered something. This works!, he said to himself. Last night he was expressing his gratitude for everything he had and that's what happened to him today. He took out the book, just to remember the sentence he read yesterday. He knew he mustn't read further, until another day had passed.

He opened the first page again and read:

By focusing on whatever form of abundance you are experiencing right now, you begin to vibrate with abundance. Even if something seemed small and unimportant at that moment. It's not true! Don't take anything for granted. By focusing on at least one thing that works for you at that moment, your focus will shift from lack to abundance. And you will feel a little better, at least for a moment. Just enough to shift your vibration.

Um.., he muttered to himself. This really works. He felt richer today than in the last two years.

He lay down on the cardboard bed and began to list his gratitudes for today.

He expressed his gratitude for meeting Zara and Heidi, the breakfast they bought for him, for taking him to a used clothes and shoes store, buying him boxers, undershirts, shoes, a blanket, for eating a hot meal in the canteen, for the possibility that he could leave his old clothes that will make someone happy, the money he had in his pocket. He was grateful that he had found a great place to sleep again, the book he was reading, how he felt today and how he this was one of his better days.

The gratitudes just kept coming. He continued to express his gratitude, until he fell asleep.

He woke up the next morning, with a smile on his face. At the same moment he remembered his dream. It was a wonderful dream. He had a house again and everything was as before. Although waking up from such a dream is painful, he was happy for this beautiful dream. At the same moment, he remembered gratitude and did his task. Gratitude made him feel good. And as he saw it for himself yesterday, the gratitude caused beautiful things. When he was done, he stood up and stretched, tucked the cardboard under his arm, put his backpack on his back and headed for the bakery to buy breakfast.

He entered the bakery and, just before he could say what he wanted, the saleswoman addressed him.

"Sir, I have a message for you. The lady who bought you food yesterday was here a while ago and left a message for you."

The saleswoman handed him a note that read:

Dear Leo!

Please meet me at eleven in the café,

next to the second-hand clothes and shoes store.

I hope to see you.

Greetings

Zara

Leo was surprised, but also happy.

"Excuse me, what time is it?", he asked the saleswoman.

"It's half past ten", the saleswoman answered him.

"Thank you! Pastries and yoghurt, please."

He took the food and headed for the café.

He arrived early and leaned against the wall across the street. He knew he shouldn't sit alone because he would be kicked out. Homeless people were not allowed to enter the café. They forced out guests and thus brought cafés into disrepute.

Leo waited patiently to see Zara.

Zara arrived after twenty minutes, right on time. Leo saw her sit down in the café's garden. She was beautiful. That woman vibrated with an incredible warmth and kindness. Today she was wearing a red coat, with a red cap on her head. She looked like some French actress. Leo crossed the road and approached her.

"Leo, I'm so glad to see you again."

"Sit down, please", Zara said, pointing to the chair next to her.

The waiter approached them cautiously, visibly confused by the scene he was witnessing.

"Ma'am, is everything OK? Is this man bothering you?"

"No sir, that's my friend", said Zara.

"We came here for a coffee."

"Okay. What are you going to drink?", continued the

waiter, but his face still showed that he was confused by the scene he was witnessing.

After they ordered drinks, Zara turned to Leo again.

"How are you, Leo? How did you sleep?", Zara asked him in such a way that Leo could feel that she really cared.

"Excellent! The blanket you bought me kept me warm all night."

"I didn't buy you anything, Heidi did", said Zara, after which they both started laughing.

"I know you must be surprised by my message to meet you, so I'll get straight to the point. Heidi and me couldn't stop thinking about you yesterday. I want to help you, if you allow me, of course."

Leo was taken by surprise. This wonderful woman left him speechless with her kindness, again.

"Before I present my proposal to you, would you like to tell me your story? How did you end up on the streets?"

Leo told her his story.

"I'm sorry to hear that. Leo", Zara said.

"I want to suggest something to you. Namely, I live alone with Heidi.

We lack a man's hand in the house. My husband no longer lives with us. We don't even know where he is because he cut off all contact with Heidi, too. We divorced a year ago and I definitely need help in the garden and, sometimes, with some chores around the house. Could you come and start working for me from tomorrow? I know it's not the job you've been pursuing so far and you can make much better use of your knowledge, but it's not a bad place to start from, right? What do you think?"

Leo was delighted. How long had he been trying to find a job. But, every time he responded to the ad, no one wanted to hire him. They told him he was unsightly or they would have lied to him that they had already found someone.

"I accept without thinking," Leo said, and they both started laughing again.

"You haven't even heard how much I would pay you per day!", Zara told him through laughter.

"I don't even need to hear it. I know it will be enough. Certainly, more than what I earn today."

They both laughed out loud again.

"I have only one condition," said Zara. That made Leo to get serious, wounded by previous experiences.

"That from this moment we are friends", Zara said quickly, noticing his reaction.

"Agreed," Leo said with a sigh of relief.

"There is no need for us to be so official. We are almost the same age, and as I can see, soon we will see each other every day."

They remained seated for another thirty minutes, which they spent in continuous conversation. Zara told him about herself and her life. She wanted them to get to know each other better so that tomorrow, when he comes, he already has the feeling that they have known each other for a long time.

"I have to go now", said Zara. "Obligations are waiting."

She took out her business card and wrote her address on the back.

"See you tomorrow at nine o'clock! Agreed?"

"Agreed!", Leo answered , once again embarrassed that he couldn't offer her a hand. He did not feel comfortable extending his dirty hand to such a lovely and decent woman.

Zara understood exactly what he intended to do and offered him her hand. Leo thanked her with a look for making him feel like a man. He held out his hand to her, and Zara couldn't stop smiling.

"See you in the morning. Heidi will be delighted that you agreed."

Zara reached for her wallet to pay the bill, but Leo stopped her with a wave of his hand.

"Allow me, madam. My treat. I just got a job."

They both burst out laughing again. Zara didn't protest because she knew how much it meant to him.

Leo left the money on the table. They greeted each other

once more and each of them went their own way.

Leo walked down the street as if in a trance. He would prefer to scream and dance in the street with happiness. However, he decided to keep his joy to himself. He also went to the canteen for lunch today. As he entered the canteen, he realized how different he was, entering there today. He's entering with confidence. He has a job! That's a big deal! He sees a way out. Now he sees the exit. He entered with a wide smile on his face and saw Martin in line. He approached him, put his hand over him and, by hugging him, told him: "Martin, today it's on me! My treat!"

He spent the day with other homeless people in the park. He didn't have to beg today. When the night fell, after a long time he went to a shelter where one night costed 10 Euro. The free shelters were already full. He could afford a bed today. And a shower. He entered a room with ten beds. He had the feeling that he had entered the most luxurious hotel. While he was waiting to take a shower, he sat down on the bed.

What a day!, he thought. What two days! He remembered that it all started yesterday.

Leo knew very well who was 'to blame' for everything. The book that promised him that his life would change. He couldn't wait to shower, lie down and continue reading.

He got into bed a few minutes later, refreshed by a warm shower and the scent of shampoo, and immediately took the book out of his backpack.

He wound the small alarm clock, which he had borrowed, for eight o'clock because he did not want to be late at Zara's.

Second step on your way towards a change, he started reading.

Two days are behind you. Hasn't the change already started, as I promised you?

What a change, Leo thought, overjoyed.

Gratitude must transform your life. It is a universal law that only people do not know. I definitely recommend that you continue to practice gratitude in your life.

Now let's move on to the second step, also unknown to many of us. A step that has as much power as gratitude. The next spell is called visualization. Visualization is what we call imagination in children. Children are still the closest to the source and their brains are still close to the alpha state and stay there the most. That's why imagination is still natural to them. They truly see what they imagine. Children see a magic wand instead of a stick they found on the floor, they see a horse instead of a broom, for them dolls are alive when they play with them. We adults don't see it, so we don't think they do either. During growing up and under the influence of adults, children also slowly come out of the alpha state and their imagination also becomes more and more distant. But it remains in us. We just need to remember it. Imagination was given to us to create life. It is a wonderful gift, an ability we are all born with.

Through visualization, we achieve the emotion of what we visualize. Many people practice it every day. And it's called worrying. Worry is nothing more than the visualization of events which we do not want to happen. So why do we imagine it? Why do we do this to ourselves? Why, in moments when bad things haven't happened yet, do we imagine they will?

Leo stopped reading because he felt the truth of these words. How much he worried, when he was deceived. And when he found out that he was deceived, he was afraid that exactly what happened would happen. That he will remain on the street, with nothing. How true is this, he thought.

It's time to turn the story to your advantage. Starting from today, instead of worrying and scaring yourself with scenarios you don't want to happen, start imagining the scenarios you want.

Visualization is a very simple process. For a few minutes a day, simply close your eyes and clearly see the realization of your wish. Live it. Feel it.

If, for example, you want a new car, with your eyes closed you see it parked in front of your house, get into it, grab the door handle, sit in it. Imagine how it looks inside, how it smells, how you ignite the engine. Hear the sound of the engine and feel the way you would really feel driving it. If you want to manifest the house of your dreams, what does your house look like from the outside? How many floors are

there, what colour is the façade, what does the entrance look like, what is the interior like, the kitchen, the living room, your bedroom, etc.? I believe you understood. The more details you can clearly see, the stronger and more stable your emotion as if you are actually witnessing it will be.

And let's remember, your emotion is your vibration. In those moments, you will send a message to the universe that this is who you are and that this is how you already live. And as I said before, you will get a reflection of yourself. Then it must come into your life. It must! We get a reflection of ourselves all the time. Now is the time to consciously manage your vibration to get what you want.

Your next task is to do visualization for the next two days. Incorporate gratitude into your mornings and evenings and, whenever you want, during the day, do the visualization as well. As many times as it suits you.

Do this exercise for two days, then continue reading. Maybe your specific desire will not come true within two days, but you will definitely have evidence that you are moving in that direction. Don't forget to notice these evidence. These are the confirmations that you are on the way make your ultimate wish come true. Notice it all, new people in your life, new events, ideas that will come to you. These are all the signs that you are on your way make your wish come true and that it is on its way.

I suggest you get excited. The magic continues.

Leo placed the book on the sideboard next to him and thought about what he had read.

Now he already believed everything he read. He just remembered himself two days ago and today. If someone had told him what would happen to him in two days, he would have declared him crazy. At that moment, he again felt gratitude towards the man who gave him the book. And at that moment, he started to list his gratitudes for today.

As he was saying them, he couldn't believe how many there were. There were now more than twenty of them. He was happiest when he expressed gratitude for his job. As he was expressing his gratitude, he was overwhelmed with emotions. He has a job! After a long time, he has a job again! And once again, at those words he was overwhelmed with gratitude. He could exactly feel its power, the power of gratitude. One of the most beautiful feelings he had ever felt. He had never been consciously grateful before in his life. He was satisfied with his life, but it cannot be called gratitude. He has never consciously stopped for a moment and realized the blessings he enjoys in his life. And he had them before. He just hasn't been noticing them.

And now, I'm going to try that visualization, he said to himself. He made himself more comfortable and closed his eyes.

He saw himself in a suit. Bathed, shaved and decently dressed. He saw himself as a businessman who vibrated with confidence and happiness. He saw himself looking in the mirror of his bedroom in the house he has again. He saw his new house. He felt his body temperature rising, while doing this exercise. He felt the warmth permeating his entire body. He felt it! He could feel now, in this moment, what that feeling would be like. He felt the tears sliding down his cheeks. These were the beautiful tears. The tears of gratitude and hope that one day he shall live it again. Even Leo himself does not know how long he did this exercise because he fell asleep while doing it.

In the morning, at nine o'clock, he came to the address that Zara had written for him. He came by bus, in which he expressed his gratitude.

A beautiful house, he thought as he approached the front door. He rang the bell.

Zara opened the door for him.

"Good morning, Leo!", she said, with a smile on her face.

"Good morning, Zara! I'm reporting for the duty", Leo said, and they both burst out laughing again. They had a similar sense of humour and it was fun for them to laugh out loud at the same time.

"Come in", said Zara.

"I have a few minutes and then I have to go."

They passed through the house towards the garden, which was located at the back of the house.

"You have a very nice house", said Leo, looking around.

"Thank you. I love it, too. And now, when the garden is maintained, it will be even more beautiful. This is my garden, as you can see. It's really big and there's a lot of work here. It would be best if you started moving dry leaves and branches today. Just cleaning it takes three days. Of course, you can maintain the pool afterwards. We shall agree on everything later. There is a guest house where you can change clothes and freshen up. I've also prepared work clothes for you. And a few more surprises", Zara winked at him. "The tools and the lawnmower are in that little house", Zara said, pointing to it. "I have to go now, I have some business, and later a parent meeting at school. Make yourself comfortable and relax, as if you were at your home. When you get tired, feel free to rest as much as you need. Do you have any questions before I go?"

"No! All clear! Just do what you have to do, and I'll get to work."

"Agreed! I'll be home until dark," she said, waving him off.

Leo entered the guest house. He put his backpack on the floor.

He saw a rich breakfast on the table. Eggs, fruit, oatmeal, milk, bread, ham and cheese, orange juice, apple juice, milk...

Everything was there. When he approached the table, he saw a message:

Dear Leo, help yourself to as much food as you like. We

know that work requires energy, so don't hesitate.

A smile spread across Leo's face.

Work clothes are waiting for you on the couch. Garden boots are outside the door. In the bathroom you have everything you need for a shower and I left you a shaver if you want to shave.

Leo unconsciously shook his head in disbelief.

Shave! If I want!? – He hasn't shaved in almost two months. He had nowhere to do that.

All towels are clean, so take whichever one you want. There are new clothes waiting for you on the bed in the bedroom (this time a gift from me, ha ha) so that you have clean clothes after showering.

Feel like at home.

See you later

Zara

Leo started to cry. He leaned his elbows on the kitchen table, buried his head in his hands and sobbed. It was as if his body could no longer handle this woman's kindness.

He felt like a man again. He felt normal. He has breakfast in front of him, a bathroom, new clothes, a shaver, a job. He has everything!

When he calmed down a bit, he sat down to have a breakfast.

He doesn't remember the last time he ate this well. He could choose. How long had he not had this kind of abundance in front of him!

When he had breakfast, he put on his work clothes and garden boots and went to get his tools.

He worked until one in the afternoon, non-stop. He took a break, during which he entered the house and ate something again. He sat down on a chair in the kitchen and took a break. He didn't want to get the couch dirty.

He did his visualization. Today, in the exercise, he imagined having his own house, like this one. How he wakes up in his bed and goes to the bathroom for his morning shower. He shaves, brushes his teeth and applies cream to his face. He puts on his bathrobe and goes to the kitchen for breakfast. He envisioned a day where he was enjoying the garden of his house and relaxing by the pool.

He was pleased to see that. He felt relaxed and happy. He did the exercise for twenty minutes. He understood exactly what the book was about. He felt emotions. He felt fantastic while doing the visualization. As if he was really experiencing it. When he finished the visualization, he went to work in the garden again. He wanted to do as much as possible to surprise Zara, but also to show her that she made a good decision to hire him.

By five o'clock, he managed to pick up and rake all the leaves in the garden. He did three days' work in one day. It was not difficult for him. In fact, he enjoyed it. He didn't know what to do with himself for too long. Leo loved to work and was never afraid of work.

He had to finish now because it started to get dark. And Zara will come soon.

He took off his boots in front of the door and headed for the bathroom.

He entered the shower, not wanting to miss the moment he was in. He doesn't have to rush. No one will knock on his door. No one else is waiting for a shower. He saw several baths on the shelf. He could choose whichever he wanted. He turned the hot water on, leaned his hands against the wall, let the water run over his scalp and head, and closed his eyes.

When he had bathed, he got out and wrapped himself in the softest towel he had ever felt. He absorbed every moment of this abundance of which he was well aware.

You're going on my gratitude list too, he said looking down at the towel, laughing to himself, at how silly this sounded.

He stood over the sink and began to shave...

Zara and Heidi arrived home. Zara saw the light in the guest house and knew that Leo was still there. She couldn't believe that she was in her garden when she saw it. All branches and leaves were removed. Leo did it all in one day.

Well done!, she thought with satisfaction, knowing that Leo would feel great about it, too. She entered the house and immediately went to change.

After about twenty minutes, Heidi and her were sitting at the table, eating the dinner she had bought on her way back.

At that moment, Leo knocked on the glass door that led to the garden.

Zara raised her head. She was left speechless. She didn't even try to hide her surprise when she saw him. He looked completely different. Combed hair and shaved beard. Only now could she see what a handsome man he was. She couldn't take her eyes off him. He was dressed in blue pants and a white shirt that she had left on his bed, and he had new shoes. Leo saw how surprised she was, so he said: "It's me, Leo!".

They both burst out laughing again.

"Leooooo!", Heidi shouted, when she saw him. "How cute you are!", said the little girl, running into his arms.

Zara pulled herself together, but she was still visibly shocked at what was hiding behind the long period of being on the streets.

"Come, join us for dinner."

Leo pulled up a chair and sat down. Zara stood up and brought him a plate.

"Take whatever you want."

They enjoyed their dinner. Heidi went to sleep and the two of them went into the living room and opened a bottle of red wine.

"What time is it?", Leo asked after what must have been more than three hours they had spent together.

"Ten past ten", said Zara, looking at her wristwatch. "I should go,"

"And how about you stay in the guest house?", Zara suggested.

"You will definitely come back tomorrow morning. There is no point in taking the bus now, sleeping over and coming back in the morning. It's more comfortable in the guest house anyway, isn't it?"

Leo was speechless again.

"Zara", he said after a few seconds of silence.

"I have no words for your kindness towards me. I don't know if I'm more embarrassed that you did everything for me in these three days or if I'm happier because of everything that's happening to me. I don't know how to repay you!"

"Leo, there's no reason to be embarrassed. What happened to you can happen to any of us. It's not your fault. I see who you are. From the first moment. Your eyes betrayed you. They told me who you were, as I saw you for the first time in that bakery. I'm really not doing anything special here. Only the things that, if the same thing happened to me, I would like someone to do for me. The guest house is gaping empty. There is no one in it. The plan is definitely for you to be here every day. Isn't it logical then that you simply move in?"

"Do you know that one day I will repay you for everything? One day I will return all this goodness I receive from you."

"I'm already getting enough from you, Leo. And we get the most by giving. And I'm really not doing anything spectacular."

"Okay. I will not refuse this offer. Thank you again, Zara."

"To the future", Zara said, raising her glass for a toast.

"To the future", Leo repeated and, looking into her eyes, knocked his glass against hers.

They were sitting and talking for some time. Zara was completely enchanted by him in this new edition. It was still the same Leo, but all evening she couldn't get over how elegant and handsome he was tonight. When they said goodnight to each other, Zara watched him as he walked through the garden towards the guest house. There was no sign of the man she saw in the bakery three days ago. And she was overjoyed about it. She knew how much it meant to Leo and how much he himself would gain even more hope now that that time was behind him

She put out the candles that were almost burnt out and went to sleep.

Leo entered the guest house and picked up his backpack from the kitchen floor. He left it there when he came this morning. He looked at that backpack, not believing how long ago it seemed to him now. He laughed, realizing that there was a blanket inside that he would no longer need. At that moment he remembered the book.

My God!, he said to himself.

Well, today I visualized that I had a house like this one! This is not possible! This afternoon I imagined it, and already in the evening, I live in it!

Okay, the house isn't mine, but...

He opened his backpack and took out the book, wanting to check if he remembered one part well.

Maybe your specific desire will not come true within two days, but you will definitely have evidence that you are moving in that direction. Don't forget to notice them.

He read this part out loud.

"Yes, that's it! I didn't forget to notice", he said out loud, proud of himself.

He sat for a few minutes in silence, thinking about all this.

Is it possible that life really works that way? That we can really create what we imagine? Why doesn't everyone know this?!, he wondered.

It doesn't matter. The important thing is that I found out, said it out loud and started laughing to himself at this sentence.

He would have preferred to continue reading the book, but he knew he couldn't for another day. He left the book on the kitchen table and went to bed.

He lay down with a smile on his face, not wanting to miss the moment in which he climbed the bed in this house. In the house of this wonderful woman, who entered his life so unexpectedly.

He started with gratitudes. Now his gratitudes were taking longer and longer. He felt fantastic doing it.

When he finished, he turned off the light, closed his eyes and began a visualization exercise.

Today he visualized having his own job. That he is his own boss. That there are a lot of workers to whom he pays wages, and that made him feel wonderful. The thought that he employed a large number of people and helped them.

He did the exercise for about twenty minutes and then fell asleep, still with a smile on his face.

Leo woke up at eight. As soon as he opened his eyes, he did his exercises from the book and took it in his hands. He can continue reading it today.

He couldn't wait. Now he already believed that the great truths of life were hidden in this book.

Welcome to the third step on your way towards a change, he started reading.

I believe that by now, at least by the slightest miracle, you have convinced yourself that everything you are reading works. Now it's time to teach you affirmations.

Affirmations mean declarations. And again, you'll see how you're actually affirming all the time, it's just that many of us are affirming what we don't want to. From today, you will start to consciously affirm the sentences you want to live. As we are able to create our lives, the affirmations we say serve to declare in advance what we want to happen in our lives!

You can start with just one sentence that you will say several times today! Convinced that it will be so! Affirmations are the most powerful if you say them in the present tense. So, not as if something is about to happen, but as if it has already happened. I'll give you a few examples:

I feel great!

Today I will witness financial abundance!

Everything I want comes true in my life!

Today is a special day!

Every cell of my body vibrates with health!

I'm a money magnet!

I believe you understand. You can find any sentence you want that describes what you want to happen.

Make that sentence your mantra. From today you can continue reading the book, whenever you want. Now you already have three tasks that you need to do every day, so that is quite enough to achieve a vibration during the day that

will bring more beautiful things into your life.

Whenever you feel ready, your affirmations can grow from one sentence to several. That depends on you. Just know that one that you will actually say is worth more than five you forget.

Leo looked at his watch. It was 8:40 AM. He had to dress slowly so that he would be ready to start work in the garden at nine. He put the book down next to him and said aloud:

Today I will witness the excellent news! Today I will witness the excellent news!

He was satisfied with the sentence he had come up with.

Today I will witness the excellent news! Today I will witness the excellent news!

He repeated this affirmation for several times.

He nodded in satisfaction and a smile spread across his face. He got up, went to the bathroom to brush his teeth, wash himself and get ready for work.

At exactly nine o'clock, knocked on the glass door of the dining room. Zara was sitting at the table drinking her morning coffee. She looked thoughtful and worried.

"Good morning, Zara! Is everything OK?"

"Good morning, Leo! Well, everything is fine, only Heidi has a cold, so I didn't take her to school, and her babysitter can't come because she went to visit her mother today. It wasn't in the plan to babysit Heidi today, so she left. And I was supposed to have two meetings today."

"I am here. Feel free to go", Leo said with a smile. "I don't want you to feel like you have to."

"Zara, I don't feel like that at all. I want to do it, and here I am. I'll be working in the garden; she'll be down here on the couch. Everything will be fine. She will be able to see me from the couch in the garden, and I will also be able to see her. Don't worry! I will go into the house every few minutes to see if she needs anything. Just tell me if something special needs to be done and consider it solved."

"Oh, that's wonderful! Thank you, Leo. I have a meeting and I was supposed to see my friend William, but I will invite him to come later."

Zara stood up, approached Leo and kissed him on the cheek.

"Thank you endlessly. I'm going to tell Heidi to get down. Count on me coming back in two or three hours."

Zara went upstairs to get Heidi, and Leo didn't move. He was completely paralysed when Zara kissed him. A wonderful energy flowed through his entire body, the likes of which he had not felt for a long time.

Is it possible that he is falling in love with this beautiful woman?

He shook his head, as if he wanted to drive those thoughts away from him, and went into the garden.

Leo and Heidi had a wonderful day. Heidi was sitting on the couch, watching TV. Leo was working in the garden and, every now and then, he entered the house and asked her if she needed anything.

When Leo finished his work, he went to the guest house to shower and change and returned to Heidi, and sat down on the couch next to her.

She just took out her school books. Regardless of the fact that she didn't go to school, she had to do her homework that she had to hand in today.

"Leo, can you help me with the fractions? I don't really like them."

"Of course! I'm an expert there", Leo replied, winking at her.

While they were solving math together, Leo didn't even notice that Zara had entered the house.

Their backs were turned to her. Zara leaned against the living room door, watching them.

What a beautiful image, she thought.

At the same moment, she felt a longing for a man in the house. Not only for myself, but also for Heidi. Heidi, unfortunately, hasn't had a male figure by her side, since her dad left. And neither had Zara. She also longed for a partner. For someone with whom she will share her life, whom she will love and who will love both her and Heidi.

She was startled by the sound of the doorbell. Leo turned suddenly and saw her at the door.

He realized that she was standing there, watching them. He just smiled gently at her, without saying anything. And Zara smiled at him.

They were looking into each other's eyes longer than usual.

The bell rang again. Zara headed towards the front door. William arrived.

"Good evening, beautiful!" said William, when Zara opened the door for him.Zara hugged him already at the door. "Come in. Thank you for coming."

"Anything for you!", said William, entering the house and handing her the bottle of wine he had brought with him.

Leo stood up to greet him and introduce himself. "William, this is Leo."

"Nice to meet you, Leo!", said William, with a big smile on his face, while reaching for Leo's hand. I've only heard the best about you.

"It's a pleasure for me, too", Leo said instantly, feeling a friendly energy from him.

"Heidi, honey, would you be so good and go on with your homework in your room?"

"Sure, Mum!", exclaimed Heidi, picking up her books from the table.

Zara went to the kitchen to open the bottle of wine she just got.

"I came to propose something to you", William said to Leo, as they sat down on the couch.

"I wanted to tell Zara about my idea first, but since I'm already here, I can tell you right away."

"Really?", asked Leo in surprise.

"Yes. Zara told me your story. And I think I can help you, too."

At that moment, Zara joined them, placing glasses in front of them and pouring wine into them.

"Leo, this is my best friend in the whole world. I believe that you will soon discover for yourself how big heart this man has."

Leo felt great. After a long time, he felt surrounded by friends and people who cared about him.

"Let's get straight to the point, so I hope we'll have something to toast to soon", William said.

"I run a small logistics company. Our speciality is the delivery of packages and parcels. The business is growing at an incredible speed day by day. And if it continues like this, I'm going to need more delivery people. When Zara told me about you and your story, I got the idea to offer you a job. What do you think?"

Leo was delighted. Another job! Before he could say anything to William, Zara started talking.

"Soon you won't have to work so many hours in the garden. An hour or two a day will be enough for maintenance, so you can do other jobs as well."

"And what can I tell you, my dears?!", said Leo, looking at William, then at Zara.

"Of course, I will accept! With both hands! But, may I suggest something? Something just dawned on me," said Leo, because he immediately remembered all those people who were spending the night outdoors.

"How about every next delivery person you hire is a person living on the streets? How about to employ people who have suffered a fate like mine? I can take on that task, if you're okay with that?"

Zara clapped her hands.

"Leo, that's a fantastic idea!" "I like it", said William.

"Work out the logistics and everything as you think it can work out and we have a deal" William said, holding out his hand.

At that moment, Leo felt incredible joy. While extending his hand, he remembered his first meeting with Zara and how he wanted to give her his hand when they were getting to know each other, but he was ashamed because he was dirty. Now he proudly extended his hand, squeezed it firmly and said: "Agreed!" Zara raised her glass, toasting to these happy news.

This moment seemed unreal to Leo, and at the same time

he was fully aware of it. At that moment he remembered that his affirmation this morning was that he would witness the great news!

This really works, he thought to himself again and started laughing out loud.

"It's time to tell you about this magical book", he told them and excitedly began to tell his incredible story.

The following months for Leo were like from the most beautiful fairy tale.

Already in the first few weeks, he devised how to logistically introduce the homeless into the business. William invested in this idea and rented a large warehouse where they built offices, where new clothes and everything for work awaited the homeless. They paid for haircuts, shaves and everything needed for the homeless to be ready for work, but also to feel like people again. As the business grew, more homeless people in the city got jobs. Soon the word about this humanitarian endeavour spread throughout the city and everyone wanted to be a part of it. The citizens started using their delivery service because they knew that they were also helping the homeless. Leo's business model began to spread to other cities.

He protected the idea as his intellectual property and soon began selling his franchise in other cities. Meanwhile, Leo and

Zara confessed their feelings to each other and lived a wonderful love.

They also bought a house. Like the one Leo visualized half a year ago. He read the book a long time ago. It changed his life completely. Not a day went by without him implementing the methods from the book. He felt as if he had discovered the greatest secret of life. He recommended everyone to read that book. He didn't want to keep that secret to himself. He always carried the book in the trunk of his new car. How many life secrets did that book reveal to him. He did not allow a day to pass without doing gratitude, visualization, affirmations. Daily meditation, which he also learned from a book, made him a calm and conscious man, as he had never been before. He lived the life of his dreams.

This morning, while he was sitting in the office, his cell phone rang.

"Mr. Leonard Turner?", he heard an unfamiliar voice on the other end.

"Yes, it's me. What can I do for you?," he asked.

"Terry Windsor on the phone. I am in your city today on business. I am interested in buying your franchise and expanding it worldwide. You are doing a very noble thing and I would like to be a part of it. Rarely does anyone come up with a logistics project like this that is financially very profitable and serves absolutely all people, not just business entities. I want to spread this to the whole world. Are you free to meet me in my office in an hour?"

"I'll be more than glad to meet you, Mr. Windsor", Leo replied, holding back from jumping for joy.

"I'll send you the address in a text message in a minute."

"Agreed! See you soon!", Leo said, taking his jacket from the chair and heading for the exit.

Leo arrived at the agreed location in forty-five minutes.

He entered the building and knocked on the office door.

"Come in, Leo!", he heard a voice from inside.

Leo opened the door and, when he saw Mr. Windsor, he was completely speechless.

My God! Is this possible?! Is this really happening?!

He never forgot this face! In front of him stood the man who had given him the book that day at the crossroads!

This moment was too much for Leo. His legs gave out completely and he fell to his knees. He cried like a little child. He cried from the wonder of this moment, the beauty of life and everything that was happening to him.

With these tears, he washed away all the difficult moments he had gone through, and at the same time he felt as if his heart was growing with love for life.

Terry walked up to him, completely confused, not understanding what was going on.

"Mr. Leonard, is everything OK? What happened?", Terry asked him, grabbing his upper arm.

Leo regained his composure, stood up and, looking at him with tears in his eyes, said:

"You have changed my life! A few months ago, at the crossroads where I was begging, you gave me a book instead of money. I was a homeless person who didn't have a cent in his pocket. And your decision to give me knowledge instead of money has brought me today to this office and this moment!"

Terry's face lit up. He remembered that moment, as well as Leo. There was no way he could recognize him, when a completely different man was standing in front of him now!

Leo stood up and hugged him tightly, continuing to cry with happiness.

Terry answered him with even tighter hug.

"Thank you, Terry! Thank you for your decision. As long as I live, I will feel gratitude towards you and what you did for me at that moment."

Leo and Terry remained so for a long time.

When Leo got into his car after two hours spent with Terry, he felt like his feet weren't touching the ground. He shook his head in disbelief at what he had just witnessed. He has just signed a contract with the man who touched his life in the most incredible way and he was about to expand his franchise to the whole world. How many homeless people will find their future and their lives will return to normal again. He knew he couldn't help every homeless person in this world, but he felt grateful for all those he could help.

He drove home, never removing the smile from his face. He couldn't wait to tell Zara what had just happened.

He suddenly startles, realizing that he's driving down the street where Terry gave him the book. He stopped at a red light, remembering that moment, when someone suddenly knocked on the passenger window.

Leo turned and saw a sad and dishevelled man through the window.

While Leo was rolling down the window, he heard:

"Sir, do you have any money for me? Please, I live on the streets and have nothing to eat."

Leo looked into his eyes and warmth spread throughout his body. He bent down, opened the compartment and pulled out a book.

Handing it to the man, he said:

"My friend, I will give you something much more valuable than what you came for. Believe me, at this moment you are not aware of how much treasure I am giving you. Greater than anything you think I could give you right now.

Please don't waste this gift! And yes, the title is a little misleading. Your life will change starting tomorrow…"

Daniel

Daniel was sitting on the bathroom floor, looking at a fist full of sleeping pills. He didn't see the pills, but the way out. A way out of the pain that has been oppressing him for too long. He just wanted to stop the pain. He tried everything, but with no success. He tried so hard not to be himself and to be different, but nothing worked. Something has been wrong with him for a long time. For fifteen years, he has been trying to be different, to be someone else, but the pain becomes unbearable. Now he already knew there was no way out. He hadn't laughed or felt joy in years. What does he need this life for? What is its purpose? He doesn't see anything to which he could hold on to. That's why today he will end all that and save himself. The pain will stop and they will feel freedom. The freedom he so passionately strives for.

He got up, poured water into a glass and took one last look at himself in the mirror.

He didn't like his reflection. A reflection of a teenager who is not like all the other, normal teenagers. It was the reflection of a teenager with whom something was wrong. That's how he saw himself. And he doesn't want to see himself like this any longer. "Never again!", he said out loud and sat down on the floor again. He remembered his mother and father who would soon find him dead on the bathroom floor. He felt no sadness. They will be relieved too, he thought. Better not to have me than to have me like this. To let them be ashamed of me.

I'm doing them a favour. This is my gift to them.

He sat for a few more minutes in silence, sorting through his thoughts that further encouraged him in his decision.

"Goodbye, world!" he said out loud.

"Neither did I enjoy you nor do I plan to stay any longer!"

He put the first pill in his mouth and took a sip of water. He repeated this until he drank all the pills. When he was done, he just leaned against the bathroom cabinet under the sink, closed his eyes, and waited for his longed-for freedom.

"Daniel, I'm home!", exclaimed Daniel's mother Linda, opening the apartment door.

She entered the apartment, taking off her shoes at the entrance and placing her purse on the hall cabinet.

"Daniel!", she called him again, wanting him to help her carry the bags to the kitchen table.

Daniel didn't respond.

She put all the bags on the floor, hung her coat on the hanger next to the front door and headed for Daniel's room.

I told him that I'll need help when I get home, and he's ignoring me, she thought angrily.

She opened the door to the room. Daniel was not there.

She knew he was in the house because his sneakers were next to the front door.

She knocked on the bathroom door, seeing that the light was on.

"Daniel, why don't you answer when I call you?!", continued the mother, still in an angry tone.

Silence. No reply.

At that moment, her anger turned down to concern.

"Daniel, I'm going in!", she said grabbing the knob, knowing that there was no key to the bathroom door.

She opened the door and instantly saw Daniel's lifeless body sitting on the bathroom floor. He was leaning against the cabinet. His head fell on his chest. Next to him were an empty glass and an empty bottle of sleeping pills.

"Daniel! Daniel!" shouted the mother, throwing herself on her knees in front of him and grabbing his head and lifting it up. Daniel didn't react.

Linda immediately put two fingers on his neck and felt a slight pulse.

"Daniel! What have you done?" shouted the mother, choking on tears.

She ran to the front door, frantically looking for her cell phone in her purse and called 911.

Daniel slowly opened his eyes. The first thing he heard was the sound of a heart rate monitor. He turned his head to the right, looking down at his hand, in which was a large needle, connected to a slowly dripping infusion. I failed, he thought disappointedly.

"Daniel, you're awake," he heard the voice of his mother, who, at that moment, jumped up from the armchair next to his bed.

"My son", his mother hugged him, crying. "You are OK. Thank God you're well."

Daniel looked at her silently. He didn't want to speak yet. He felt tired. And disappointed.

"Oh, we're awake," he heard the nurse who entered the room at that moment.

"Rest today and you can go home tomorrow", said the nurse, changing the infusion bottle.

Daniel did not react. He stared into the distance, not wanting to face what awaited him now.

I can't even kill myself! Well, what a loser I am!, he thought, and the tears began to flow down his cheeks.

"Son, all is well, my son! All is well now!", said Linda, his mother, seeing that he started to cry.

The nurse changed the infusion bottle and, on her way out, said to Daniel's mother: "Go home tonight. You didn't rest properly for three days. Don't worry about him, he's safe here."

"Daniel, my son, you scared us a lot. Why, honey? What

happened so terribly that you decided to do what you did?"

"You wouldn't understand that, mum! No one understands me", answered Daniel quietly.

"But, son, nothing is so terrible that it cannot be solved! But that's irrelevant now, we have all the time in the world to sort everything out. Come on, rest now and we'll go home tomorrow."

Linda leaned over him, kissing him on the forehead. "I'll see you in the morning and then we'll go home."

When Daniel and Linda entered the apartment the next morning, David, Daniel's father was sitting on the couch.

He was cold and distant. Daniel was used to him like that. He knew, from his first steps, what the army had done to his father. He was a typical soldier. Cold, bossy and focused on achievement. Daniel knew that his father wanted him to follow his footsteps because it would be an honour for him. Daniel, not only didn't want that, but he was hiding a secret that would devastate his father.

He knew his father loved him, but Daniel wanted to be loved in a different way. He so desperately wanted his father to love him for who he was, not for what his father thought Daniel would become.

"Sit down, Daniel!", said the father, pointing to the couch.

Linda did not want to get involved because she already knew her husband well enough, and sometimes it was terribly difficult for her herself because of his coldness towards their son. And she so wished that his father had hugged him now and shown how scared he was for him, but she knew that his walls were too high and that he was showing love in the only way he knew how.

Daniel sat down without saying a word, looking at the floor.

"Are you even aware of what you tried to do?"

"Yes", answered Daniel, knowing that this was the best way to talk to his father.

"Can we get an answer as to why you decided to do that?"

Daniel was silent. If his father only knew how many times he mustered up the courage to tell him and never succeeded. How many years has his truth been screaming inside him, but it has never come out.

"Daniel, you have embarrassed this family. The whole town is talking about you. I've been trying my whole life to make a real man out of you. A strong man! And you behave like a coward. Only weaklings do what you tried to do. They run away. What, some girl dumped you and it's the end of the world? Is that the reason? Real men face everything life throws at them. And win!"

"Well, perhaps I'm not a real man!", shouted Daniel through tears, ran to his room and slammed the door.

The mother also shed tears.

"Don't be so harsh with him!", she told her husband.

"Are you aware of how sensitive he is now? Do you really want us to lose him?"

Daniel's father looked at his mother, as if he only realized what he was doing at that moment.

"But I want to strengthen him! I want him to understand that he must be strong through life! Life is not easy. To no one, also not to him. What would happen if we all tried to kill ourselves when it was difficult?! None of us would make it to adulthood. Does he even know what I went through as a child? With an alcoholic father and an illiterate mother who had no right to speak for herself. That's why I chose to join the army. To prove to everyone, especially to my father, that I will never be like him and that I am stronger than his beatings and humiliations. To prove him that he was wrong when he was telling me that I was nobody!"

"But Daniel is not you. He is himself. You can't expect him to be like you. Don't you see how many years you've been trying to make yourself out of him and you're constantly failing at this. I guess that is telling you something."

"We will finish this conversation now," said Daniel's father, going into the hallway, from which he took his jacket and left the house.

Daniel heard a knock on his room door.

"Honey, may I come in?", his Mum asked, opening the door. Daniel sat on his bed, in total silence.

His mother sat down next to him, reaching out for his hands.

"Son, you have to talk to me. I need to know the reason for your decision to end your life. What is happening without us knowing?"

If she only knew how much he wanted to tell her what was going on inside him for many years, for how long he had been fighting it. And how was he supposed to tell her that? How could he put that burden on their backs? It's too hard for him, too.

"Mum, you wouldn't understand", answered Daniel quietly.

"Why are you saying that, my son? How do you know I won't understand it, if you don't try? I am your mother and I will love you forever, no matter what. Why do you think you can't tell me what it's about?"

"Because I will disappoint you, Mum, not to mention Dad." My whole life he has expectations of me, which I can't possibly fulfil."

"I'm not talking about your father now, nor is he here now. I'm here, telling you that there is nothing you can't tell me that will make me stop loving you. Your heart beat beneath mine. I carried you inside my womb for nine months. You are a part of me. The most beautiful part of me, Daniel. You need to talk to me. How can I help you, if you don't want my help?"

"Mum, please believe me! Give me some time to sort out my feelings. I promise we'll talk about everything soon. I am very tired. I don't have the strength for anything now. I would like to go to sleep."

"Okay, son. Take a rest. Tomorrow is school. And a new day!", said his Mum, kissing him on the cheek.

When she left the room, Daniel lay down, exhaled deeply and pulled the blanket over his head.

He entered school with his head down. He had the feeling that everyone was looking at him. Everyone knew. But no one approached him. They were just whispering to each other, pointing fingers at him.

He sat down at his desk, trying to ignore everyone around him.

Professor Thomas entered the classroom and immediately looked at Daniel. Daniel noticed his look. He loved that history professor, who loved all of them. All the students adored him. He was a professor who always saw them as they were. He saw people, not the disciples in them. Because of him, everyone fell in love with history. He turned every lesson into a play and turned history into life lessons. No class of his went by, without him instilling in them some life lesson that will serve them in the future. He was an artist who would lead them from the history lesson to their future.

"Good morning, my dearest generation!", said Professor Thomas with a smile, to which the whole class laughed because that was how he used to greet them every class, and not only their class, but every class he entered. And everyone knew that, but they would feel special again, if he said it to them.

"I have a present for you today! Although many people think that it is more important to fill their heads with information, I know otherwise. It is more important to fill the heart. Because when you fill it up, the most important thing remains in your head. What remains is the knowledge of how to live life! Today we will also talk about history, but your history, the one that has a more important meaning for you than the history of Babylon, where it was and what happened to it."

The whole classroom was filled with laughter, followed by a loud applause.

"Prepare paper and pen. And when you're done with the task, you can go out for a break."

"Yesss!", it was heard from the last bench!

There was a murmur in the class, as they opened their bags and tore a paper out of their notebooks.

"Okay", said Professor Tomas, when he saw that everyone was ready.

"You will write an essay entitled WHO WAS I AND WHO WILL I BECOME"

"Write as much as you want. No rules. The purpose of the essay is to recall your past and conclude whether it affects your future. Not only does it affect you, but also how does it affect you? And yes, you don't need to sign if you don't want to. In fact, it is more interesting that way. Your first and last names have nothing to do with it anyway and I don't care what your name is. I'm interested in who you are, when you describe yourself without an identity. You can start and when you're done, bring the essay to my desk and you can go out for a break."

The students got to work. In complete silence. In the classroom where Professor Thomas taught, there was always respect in the air. The students respected him because he respected them.

Professor Thomas sat down at his desk and secretly, through his glasses, looked towards Daniel.

Daniel didn't see him. He was looking at the paper, preparing to start writing.

He began to write, deeply engrossed in the task.

As time went on, every now and then one of the students would finish, put the pen on the table and bring the essay to the professor's desk. They were leaving the classroom in silence. After about thirty minutes, the penultimate student came out. Only Daniel and Professor Thomas remained in the classroom.

Daniel was still writing. Professor Thomas pretended to read the newspaper, not to make Daniel uncomfortable. He didn't read the newspapers. He was thinking about Daniel, who he had been thinking about since the moment he heard that he had tried to take his own life. He spent the whole weekend thinking about how to help this beautiful boy to free himself from the shackles that were pressing him so hard and dragged him to the bottom.

That's why he was delighted, when he came up with the idea of an essay that would make the other students leave the classroom, without everyone realizing how much he wanted to be left alone with Daniel. Calling Daniel into his office in front of the other students could be disastrous for Daniel as he could feel the additional shame because of everything that happened. He was already in the focus of all the students, and Professor Thomas didn't want to cause him additional stress.

The bell rang. Daniel winced.

"It's okay, Daniel!", Professor Thomas tried to calm him down.

"Take your time. Today we have block class anyway. You still have time.

We are in no hurry."

"Professor, is anyone going to read this but you?", Daniel asked him quietly.

"No, Daniel. No one except me."

"And are you going to tell anyone what we wrote?" "No,

this is between me and you."

Daniel broke down at that moment. Whether it was from the relief or the weight of the burden he's carrying, Professor Thomas had yet to discover.

The professor stood up, walked over to Daniel, leaned over his desk, put his arm over his shoulder and pulled him into a hug.

Daniel began to cry even louder.

"Cry, Daniel, feel free to cry. Get out of yourself all the pain you 're carrying with you. You are safe here. I'm here. On your side."

Daniel was crying uncontrollably. The tears soaked the paper that was all written on.

Professor Thomas let him cry out his pain and rinse his aching soul.

After a few moments, when he saw Daniel calm down a bit, he pulled a chair next to his and sat down.

"Daniel, do you know who I am?"

"I know, my professor", Daniel answered , wiping his nose and eyes with his sleeve.

"And your best friend at the moment," the professor continued.

Daniel was looking into his eyes now. How much he wanted a friend. Someone to whom he can tell everything. Someone who will not judge him, but who will support him. And he had no one.

"Do you trust me?"

"I do", Daniel answered.

"You know, we professors are not here just to teach you lessons we usually teach you. We have chosen this invitation to guide you. To see your potential that you don't see yet. And even if it's not a subject we teach. Nor should it be. Not everyone is interested in history, nor will they ever need information from history in their lives. A professor should know this and, by teaching, notice where the light burns in you. See which road that flame in you lights up. But above all, to see in you the young people who want to live happy lives. And a professor must never forget that.

I haven't forgotten. And I won't. Never. And that's why I'm telling you this now. I'm here to help you to be happy. But you have to help me. Your life is like being the captain of your ship. The ship does not sail alone, you're steering it. I am like a lighthouse. I will help light your way, guide you, but you're steering the ship, remember that! I can't help you if you don't tell me what it is that's bothering you. And know that it will stay between us. I promise you that. Unless we decide together that it's time for someone else to find out."

Daniel silently handed him the paper. "Everything is written there", Daniel said quietly.

"Read it to me," the professor said, pushing the paper back

to Daniel.

"That's your truth, say it out loud. Until you speak your truth out loud and accept it as your own, it remains hidden from you, the world and life. Never resist life. And don't fight it because it always wins! And it should win. Because life is you! You can't beat yourself, you can only live yourself! And if you managed to escape from life, you know what would have happened to you? You would live it all over again. Everything would be the same. Because you didn't do the lesson you came for. You were not who you truly are. Your soul would know that and make the same choice again. That's why it's better to learn to rise from the pain and sadness, than to go through this road all over again."

"What do you mean when you say that my soul knows what choice I've made?", Daniel was confused.

"Daniel, you are much more than your body. You are not a body that has a soul. You are the soul that chose to have this body and everything that this body carries. We all come into this world choosing what we will be and what kind of life we will live. We come to learn about ourselves, to grow, to get to know each other. This journey of ours should strengthen us, and those who find the road in the most difficult way realize their strength and power at their highest. We are not here to fight life; we are here to remember who we are. Our life is our greatest ally in this."

"And what if we don't like who we are?", Daniel asked .

"It means you still haven't understood life. And that's fine. It's a process. That is why it is designed to last a long time. Now let me hear what you wrote in your essay. Let's go together on this journey of yours."

Daniel sighed deeply and brought the paper closer.

"Who Was I And Who Will I Become", Daniel read the title and started:

"I don't remember ever being happy" he read.

"Neither when I was a baby, neither when I was a boy. Okay, maybe I was happy as a baby, but I don't remember that. The first thing I remember is that I was different from my childhood. The other children didn't like me and didn't want to play with me. I didn't like going to kindergarten because I had no friends. My father never liked me. Never. He doesn't like me even now. I know he would like me to be someone else. When I was thirteen, I realized what was wrong with me. I fell in love for the first time. I wasn't sure what being in love looked like, but I had a feeling that this was it. Because it gave me a good feeling. But terrible at the same time. Because something abnormal was happening. I fell in love with a boy, with whom I was sitting in the classroom. Patrick."

Daniel stopped reading and looked at Professor Thomas, as if he wanted to see if Professor Thomas understood that it was Patrick who still attends school with him and whom he also teaches.

"Just keep going, don't worry, everything is well," said the

154

professor, putting his hand on his shoulder in an attempt to encourage him, without giving him the slightest sign that he understood who it was.

"I didn't want it, it just happened. Girls didn't exist for me. They didn't cause any emotion in me. And when I saw him and was close to him, my whole body seemed to be happy. Only then was I happy. On one occasion, we were left alone at my house and I touched his hand. He looked at me the same way I looked at him. I knew, at that moment, that he felt the same way. That gave me the strength to kiss him. When my lips touched his, he didn't protest at first, but then he pushed me away and shouted: "Are you normal?! Get away from me!", and ran home. I cried that whole day and night. The next day, when I came to school, I was convinced that he would demand to sit wit with someone else, but that didn't happen. He would hold my hand under the desk. When we were alone in the school bathroom, he would kiss me for a second and leave. All the time he was sending me signals that he liked me too. But only when we were alone. When he was with his friends, he would mock me, tease me and pretend that we were not friends. This lasted for several months. Then he started dating a girl from his class and nothing was clear to me. He still gave me attention when we were alone. He once told me that I shouldn't tell anyone what was going on between us. That this is not normal and that the whole school will make fun of us. That he will beat me if I tell anyone. That this is a secret we must take with us to the grave. I was broken. Scared, in love and broken. I wanted so badly that we didn't have to hide, but that wasn't an option for Patrick. And over time, I also realized that no one should find out who I am. I didn't see him the whole summer, and when the new school year started, he pretended he doesn't know me. And I saw that he goes into the toilet alone with another boy and that he is now doing everything with him that he did with me. I ceased to exist for him. I googled all the time what was going on with me and why I liked a man and of course realized what was wrong with me. I'm gay!"

At that moment, Daniel stopped reading, without looking up. That was the last sentence he wrote.

Professor Thomas looked at him with a gentle expression, without any judgement. Daniel felt it, too. He felt that this wonderful professor did not judge him.

"Daniel, just because you're not like the most of the boys doesn't mean there's something wrong with you. You're just different from most of your peers. And that's perfectly fine. It does not mean that you are broken, sick or anything else. It means that you are simply different. And being different doesn't necessarily mean something bad. In fact, those who are different are rare. Those who are different stand out from the majority, and the majority is average. All excellent people have never been average."

"But everyone would judge me for that."

"People judge what they don't understand. They don't even realize that they are judging because they are afraid, and you know what they are afraid of?"

"Of what?"

"Of their own ignorance. That scares them. Not that someone is different, but that they have no idea what that means and how to deal with it. Then they hide their ignorance behind loud attacks on the others. By judging and insulting those different from them, they falsely give themselves importance, and deep down they are small. Their ignorance makes them small. Because knowledge gives you greatness. Knowledge is power."

Daniel was listening to him carefully.

"I have tried everything not to be like this." "I believe you have. And how are you doing?"

"Well, not good at all."

"There you see! And it will never work for you. Trying to be what you are not is a game without limits. Which is very exhausting. Is that why you tried to take your own life?"

"Yes. I had the feeling that I couldn't cope with this any longer. It hurt too much."

"It's time to start living who you truly are. I told you a while ago that you made the choice of who you will be before you were born. You knew exactly what was waiting for you and what kind of environment you were coming to, but it was more important for you to come for this experience where you will learn a great lesson."

"Which one?"

"Love is love. It has no limits. It has neither gender nor sex. It is simply love."

"Do you know how strong a soul you really are?"

"Me? Strong?", Daniel asked with a cynical smile.

"If I'm not something, I'm not strong."

"Oh, but you are! You see, most people's souls choose to feel love for people of the opposite sex throughout their lives. And that path is easy because it is normal in this world. And now imagine the courage and strength of your soul. It knew that it was making a choice that was different from the majority, a choice that would be welcomed by condemnation and misunderstanding, but it still said *yes* to that choice! Isn't that soul very brave?"

Daniel smiled to himself. He liked what he heard.

For the first time, someone said something about being gay, without making him feel bad and less valuable.

"Do your parents know who you really are?", Professor Thomas continued.

"No! Nobody knows. That would kill my parents. Especially my father. My father has been a soldier all of his life. Imagine if I told him that. That would kill him. I even think he would give me up."

"Why are you so sure of that?"

"Because all his life he has been trying to make a man out of me, a soldier, himself. He has never accepted me for who I am. I can't imagine what would happen, if he knew about this."

"I'll talk to him" ,Professor Thomas said.

Daniel didn't protest. Yes, he was afraid of his father's reaction when he found out, but he did not protest. He was tired of resisting.

"Daniel, you must tell your parents clearly and loudly who you are and what is bothering you. How can they help you if they don't know what it's about? I'm sure your mother is also suffering deeply because she doesn't know what's happening to you and why you tried to kill yourself. Your father can only be in fear at that moment, but in fear of his ignorance, as I explained it to you. Let me explain it to him. All will be well, trust me. You have to take that burden off yourself. Otherwise, it will become too heavy again. And remember what I told you. If you succeed in your plan to take your own life, you will come again and go through all of this from the beginning. Let's rather continue it now from here, to where you have already come. And you've come a long way. You can do it, you're not alone. I am with you."

"Okay", Daniel said. Although he was afraid, he felt that he would not be alone on this journey.

Professor Thomas stood up and took out a piece of paper from his notebook and wrote:

Dear Mr. and Mrs. Bennet,

I will be free tomorrow at 5 PM to come to talk to you

Regards

Prof. Thomas Coleman

"Go and take a break now, Daniel. See you tomorrow. All will be well."

Daniel came home after school. His mother was preparing dinner, and his father was watching TV in the living room. He went into his room, feeling different than this morning. It was as if he was relieved to have revealed his secret to someone. It was as if part of the burden he was carrying fell off his shoulders.

"Danieeeeeel, dinner!", he heard his mother calling him.

He reached into his school bag and took the paper Professor Thomas had given him and headed towards the dining room.

When both father and mother sat down at the table, Daniel handed the paper to his mother. "They gave me this at school to give it to you", he said.

The father raised his head towards him and then towards his wife, waiting to hear what she's going to read.

Dear Mr. and Mrs. Bennet,

I will be free tomorrow at 5 PM to come to talk to you

Regards

Prof. Thomas Coleman

Daniel's mother read the letter aloud.

"What have you done?", his father asked.

"Nothing", Daniel answered.

"There's a reason he wants to talk to us."

"Well, there is, but I haven't done anything wrong. He said he wanted to talk to you."

"Of course, we will talk to him" his mother said.

"It doesn't even matter why now; we'll find out tomorrow."

"Tell me, Daniel, how was school today?", his mother continued talking to him.

Daniel and his mother were talking at the table about the day that had passed. He didn't tell her about the essay or what happened with Professor Thomas. He didn't have the strength for it yet. The father sat at the table the whole time, not saying a word.

When he finished dinner, Daniel was the first to get up from the table and go to his room.

"Why are you like that towards him?", the mother asked the father.

"Cold and unapproachable. Do you know how sensitive he is now? You didn't say a word to him the whole evening."

"And what should I do, so who is the father here and who is the son?!", he asked angrily. "I guess he is the one who should address me first!"

The mother sighed deeply.

She knew how much Daniel cries out for his father's love, but also how cold his father can be. And she knew that deep down he wasn't like that. And that's why it hurt her even more. And she didn't know how to help both of them to establish a good relationship.

"Fine," she said, as if surrendering.

"Nothing, I'm going to sleep. Count on Professor Thomas coming tomorrow at five."

At exactly five o'clock, the doorbell rang. Daniel opened the door and saw Professor Thomas.

"Good afternoon, Daniel", the professor greeted him.

"Are your parents expecting me?"

"Yes, come in. Just straight to the living room."

His mother and father met him on their feet, extending their hands towards him and greeting him.

"Welcome", Daniel's father greeted him. "Please sit down."

Mother took the professor's coat, carried it into the hallway and hung it next to the front door.

"What would you like to drink?", she asked him.

"One cup of coffee will be fine", the professor said.

"It'll be here in a minute."

"How are you, Professor?", Daniel's father asked him, not wanting to create an awkward silence.

"I'm great! Thank you for asking. How are you?"

"Listen, how can I be considering what we lived through the other day?!"

At that moment, the mother entered the living room, carrying coffee for the professor.

"Here you go", she politely addressed the professor, placing a cup of coffee, milk and sugar on the table.

She sat down next to her husband, visibly tense, expecting to find out the reason for the professor's visit.

"Thank you", Professor Thomas said.

"It smells wonderful... I totally understand how you feel. That is the reason for my visit today. I would just like to ask you, Daniel", he said addressing him, "to leave us alone for a few minutes, and you can join us later."

Without a word, Daniel got up and headed for his room. It didn't matter to him that he didn't know what the professor was going to talk about with his parents, but at the same time he trusted him.

When the professor heard the door to the room close, he continued.

"I came with the desire to help you understand the reasons for his decision to take his own life."

"You know the reason", said the mother worriedly.

"Yes", he told me yesterday.

"And, which one is it?", continued the father, still showing no emotion of any kind.

"Before I tell you, I would like to talk to you. Do you love your child?", asked the professor.

"Of course, we love him", answered the mother.

"And what about you? Do you love him?", the professor asked Daniel's father, who did not answer his question at first.

"The answer to that question should be clear, shouldn't it?", replied the father.

"But it is not clear. That's why I'm asking you. I'm not here to tell you that you don't love him, but to help you figure out if you love him the way needs to be loved. How do you know you love him?", continued the professor, looking at Daniel's father.

"Because I only wish him the best in life. I want him to be a fighter who will not be broken by anything. That he knows how to deal with life and everything that life brings."

"You listed everything you want for him and everything that should happen in the future. Many parents, worrying about who their child will become, forget they are already someone today. Do you love him today? Now? Who is he now?"

Daniel's father remained silent for a while, then said:

"For me, the focus is now on who he will become. That's how we were taught in the army. A soldier, when he joins the army, is not even close to what he will become. And we are preparing him today for tomorrow."

"Your son is not a soldier, and parenting is not supposed to be a military, right? Daniel tried to take his own life. Doesn't it seem to you that this method is not effective? You were close to losing the soldier you were waiting for. Daniel needs your love now. He cries out for your acceptance. Not only him, every child wants it. For the parent to see and hear him."

Daniel's father nodded his head in approval.

"I came to tell you that I spoke with him. I assigned all students the task of writing an essay entitled WHO AM I AND WHO WILL I BECOME. Daniel wrote in it the reasons why he is unhappy and due to which the burden he feels has become too heavy for him. I will let you read it now. I am just asking you not to judge him and to be open-hearted, not forgetting for a moment that your child's life is at stake here. He needs your support. You'll either help him be who he is or, believe me, he won't be among us."

Professor Thomas handed them Daniel's essay. Mother took it and put it in front of her and father and they started reading it together.

Professor Thomas leaned back in his armchair, sipping his coffee. He observed them as they were reading it.

The tears flowed down his mother's cheeks, while the father's expression was not changing.

When they read the essay to the end, they both remained silent, not knowing what to say.

No one prepared them for this scenario.

"Daniel is a wonderful boy", professor Thomas broke the awkward silence.

"A wonderful boy who is different from most of his peers, but only in that he feels emotions towards the same sex. Some people are simply born that way. And that is a part of him, his personality and identity. And when you're like that, it's natural to you and you're not able to fight it. And you wouldn't fight against it, if the world didn't force you to. And now imagine how he feels when he knows that he is different from the majority, and that the majority does not accept him. Imagine that for two people who should be the biggest support in his life, he feels that they are not there. He lives in constant fear. Can you imagine such a life? It presses and suffocates you every second of the day. You have no one to talk to about it, no one to comfort you, encourage you, help you along the way. And what is he doing wrong? Nothing. Not a single step. He just wants to live and love."

"Can we call him now, please?", asked the mother, still wiping the tears from her face.

"Of course,", said Professor Thomas.

"Daaaaaniel!", his mother called for him.

She heard the door to the room open. Daniel timidly appeared at the door of the living room, not knowing how much his parents knew about him now.

"My son!", his mother said,, standing up and hugging him.

"My son, you don't know how much I love you. All is well. All! I'm sorry that you couldn't tell us what's bothering you, what you're feeling and what you're going through."

Daniel began to cry loudly. He hugged his mother tightly, relieved that they finally knew.

The father still sat there, as if struggling with his thoughts and feelings.

"Daniel, you'll let me pull myself together. This is a big shock for me", he finally said.

"I was ready for everything in life, but not for this", said the father, getting up from the armchair.

"Professor, excuse me. I'm going to take a walk and pull my thoughts together."

Professor Thomas held out his hand and Daniel's father walked towards the exit door, put on his jacket and left the house.

"Come Daniel, sit with us", his mother invited him to join them.

At that moment, the professor's cell phone rang.

"Excuse me. I have to answer this."

Then he went to the kitchen.

The mother was still hugging Daniel tightly, when Professor Thomas returned to the living room. His expression became extremely serious and worried.

"The school principal just called me. Our student Patrick Bale committed suicide today at two o'clock in the afternoon."

Daniel felt that he was losing the ground under his feet. Patrick?! Patrick?! Not him! Why? He had the feeling that he was dreaming. This is not true, he heard something wrong.

He started crying uncontrollably. His mother was also shocked by the news. She didn't know Patrick, but she instantly remembered Patrick's mother and thought how she was feeling right now.

"Excuse me. I have to go to school. They will call you soon. They want all students and parents to come to the school hall at nine in the morning. Thank you for receiving me. And once again, convey my greetings to your husband."

There was silence in front of the school that morning. The school flag was at half-mast. Children and their parents came from all sides, entering the entrance to the hall.

Daniel arrived with his parents at five minutes to nine and they all sat together in the front row.

There was a murmur in the hall, but it wasn't a happy murmur, as it usually happens when school games or competitions are held.

The professors walked into the hall exactly at nine o'clock. One by one, they entered in silence and sat on the chairs lined up on the stage. Everyone was silent.

The school principal stood behind the pulpit and, at that moment, a photo of Patrick appeared on the big screen behind him. Patrick was smiling on the photo. He looked happy. Now the whole school knows that it was only a mask that protected him and with the help of which he survived from day to day.

"Dear students and parents", the principal began with his speech.

"Unfortunately, we did not gather today as usual, when we support the athletes of our school. When we encourage them and cheer for them and their successes. Successes that will enable them to have a bright future. Today we gathered because of a sad act, because of the decision of one of our students to abruptly end his young life. Our dear Patrick who will not have the chance to experience a bright future. We invited you all because Patrick, although he decided to end his life, did not want to go in vain. He wanted, if he could not continue this life, that this should not happen to anyone in this school again, and that is why he left his last words and wish in the form of a message."

Although not a single voice was heard in the hall, there was a reaction to the director's words.

Many parents and students cried.

Patrick's final message to all of you will now be read by Professor Thomas.

Professor Thomas stood up, holding a paper in hand, and approached the pulpit and microphone.

"Greetings from me too, dear children and parents. I asked the director that I should address you with a few words and read Patrick's last words to you. I wanted it to be me for a number of reasons. I have been working in this school for 20 years. I welcomed and escorted numerous generations. What I have never done and what I would never allow myself, no matter how many children have passed through my classroom and no matter how many years I have been in school, is to take children for granted. To become just a number in my diary. I respect each of you, my children, deeply and individually, and each of you is equally important to me. But why? Because I know how important you are to yourself. How, no matter how many children are around you, you look at life through your eyes, feel your emotions, desires, worries, fears. Each of you goes to bed every night and is alone with themselves. With their thoughts. And that's how I see you too. That's how I see you today. And that is why I am asking you now to truly hear this message Patrick left for you. To listen to her, knowing that this boy was also like that. Every day, when he came home from school, he was left alone. Alone with himself, his thoughts, emotions, desires, worries and fears. And it all became too difficult for him. Every day, when he came home from school, he was left alone.

But who Patrick truly was is not shown by the act he did, but by this message he left to all of us. And don't remember him as a boy who took his own life, but as a boy who, with his last message, wanted to make life nicer and easier for all of us."

Everyone in the hall was crying. Patrick's mother, who was sitting in the first row, surrounded by Patrick's sisters, was loudest.

And Professor Thomas could barely hold back his tears, but he knew he had to be strong and read the message Patrick left behind him. It was more important for him at this moment to convey this powerful message, and he would deal with his pain later.

Patrick's mother, who was sitting in the first row, surrounded by Patrick's sisters, was heard the loudest.

I am writing this message a few moments before I'm about to leave this world. A world that has never accepted me. My whole life was one big lie. A lie that has become so heavy for me that I don't want to live it any longer. All I wanted from life was to be able to be who I truly am. And I failed in that. I tried everything not to be like this, but I failed. And when I dared and encouraged myself to show everyone who I am, someone always reminded me that who I am is not valid and not normal. I am writing this message to address you all now, when I have the courage. Because by the time you will be listening to this, I will be gone. No one will be able to hurt me or mock me or threaten to beat me. I will

be free. But I'm not writing this just for myself. I'm writing for all of you who stay. Because of those who caused me pain, but also those who feel the pain.

I am writing because of all of you who have led me to this act with your actions.

Who do you think you are, if you bully those weaker than you around school, you make fun of them so that the whole school laughs at them. No! You are not big shots; you are the exact opposite! I want to address you first.

Being strong means having so much strength that you can help lift up someone who needs strength at that moment. You do your violent act and go about your day, not realizing how much you break the other person, how much you weaken his spirit. You leave forgetting about us, and we think about you for hours, days and months. Some of you, for a whole life. Because you broke us so much that we can never stand up again.

There was dead silence in the hall. Everyone, breathless, listened to what Professor Thomas was reading, and you could clearly see who was bowing his head and recognizing himself in these words.

Stop doing that, please! Stop looking at us different from you, as unimportant people because we are not. We are people like you. Different in something. So what? Why do we all have to be like you? Who made you the standard that the

172

only right thing is what you are. Because it's not. Especially not when you bully and abuse others. You are the exact opposite of that. The opposite of everything I would ever want to be. I'm not writing this message to make you feel bad because that's what you did to me and I don't want to be the same as you. I'm writing you this message in case you don't understand what you're doing. Maybe for the first time in my life. To understand and never do it again. To remember me, who never did anything bad to you, and you weakened me, so much so that I no longer have the strength to go on. You will see tomorrow, I won't. In a few years you will be putting on your suits, picking up your girlfriends and entering the school hall for the prom, I won't. You will experience love and have families, I won't. And that will be the only difference between us. You will get on with your life, I won't. Because of people like you. And that's why the next time you start mocking someone, hitting and humiliating them for no reason, remember these words. Your actions have far greater consequences than you realize. And they're not funny. Not at all.

You want to be strong? Be strong enough to accept those different from you. That's strength! To accept what you may not understand.

Now that I'm gone, for the first time I can say it loud and clear: I'm gay! I was falling in love with men! And I only felt what we call love towards men!

Professor Thomas deliberately stopped reading for a

moment, not only to give strength to these words, but also to see the reactions of everyone listening to this.

The surprise on the faces of many students was clearly visible. They looked at each other, as if they were asking if this was true. Many of them have never thought that Patrick was gay. Exactly the opposite. He always had girlfriends and acted like a big shot. The faces of several students showed that they were not surprised because they were the ones who suspected that this was so and because of that they teased Patrick and bullied him. Those students bowed their heads.

Patrick's mother did not react because Patrick left a note for her and his sisters in which he wrote this to them.

Daniel remained speechless. Daniel knew. He had a crush on him in elementary school and they kissed secretly But he also knew that Patrick never wanted to admit it publicly and how much he convinced him that he can never admit publicly that he loves men.

Now that I have said this publicly for the first time and you have heard this from me for the first time, I want to address the parents, Professor Thomas continued reading Patrick's message.

Be there for your children. As soon as possible. Talk to them. Get them to tell you the truth that lives within them. But you cannot bring them to that point with condemnation, threats and criticism. They need to feel safe, no matter what they tell you. Your children go through all kinds of things

at school. Things you will never know if you just ask them about grades. School is much more than grades. School makes or breaks us.

And your task is to help us. My mother is now listening to these words of mine and will never have the chance to talk to me again. Don't let that happen to you.

At that moment, Daniel's father lowered his head and placed his hand on his forehead. He heard these words clearly. For the first time, his emotions could be clearly seen.

Daniel noticed that. He felt a glimmer of hope.

Don't expect your children to be what you want them to be. That's not your task. Your task is to help us become who we want to be. There are no beatings, punishments and criticisms that will change us. Guide and direct us with your love. Accept who we are. That's all we want. For you to see and hear us! Do you want us to be successful? No! You want us to be happy! Happy people become successful. Unfortunate people become low lives who constantly struggle with life.

And that's why I'm asking you, if I want anything at the end of my life, to be with your children so they don't feel alone. Let my sadness be an example for your children and that it is a better solution to accept them as they are, than to be left without them. Because you will! The pain we carry often becomes too much for us. It became to me. Don't let it happen to your child.

At this moment, Daniel's father put his hand over his shoulder.

And finally, I would like to address one special person. To the person whom I hurt a lot with my fears and insecurities. And I know he is today among you. The burden of life is also becoming too heavy for him.

I won't name him because I don't want to put him in a situation he may not be ready for.

He will know who he is. My first love, my first kiss with a man.

Daniel held his breath. He knew he was talking about him.

Please forgive me for the pain I caused you. I was scared. Scared because of how I felt about you. My harsh words to you were a reflection of my pain and my fear. Don't listen to what I told you. Don't be ashamed of yourself and be proud of yourself. You are a wonderful being and you have always been good to me. Love! Love without any reserves. You gave me more love than all the girls after you. Don't hide your truth any longer! Those who do not understand you should not be a part of your life. Live love, the way you feel love should look like for you. Isn't it better to love than to live in fear of love all your life? Don't let happen to you what happened to me. And I want these words to be my gift to you. To give you hope and strength to live your truth. Because living your truth means living love!

Before I say goodbye to you once and for all, I have just one more wish. All of you who have come today to hear my words and to pay my respects and last greetings in some way, do it in such a way as to accept this person! Give him the strength to publicly show who he is and to feel the support he has never felt in his life. That for the first time in his life he feels that you see and hear him. To feel pride for who he really is for the first time in his life! If you want to give me something for the end, give it to someone who is like me.

Professor Thomas folded the paper to indicate that it was the last sentence.

At that moment, applause was heard in the hall. First a few people, and then more and more, until the whole hall was filled with applause of support. Everyone was clapping and looking to see which student it was and if something was going to happen.

Daniel was breathing rapidly, gathering his strength for what was to come. He knew that this was a decisive moment in his life. Now or never, he said to himself. He stood up and at the same moment everyone turned towards him. The applause became even louder. And shouts of support. The tears started rolling down Daniel's face. He felt like he had never felt. For the first time in his life, he felt what is like to be finally free.

He looked towards the stage. All the professors stood up and also applauded to support Daniel. Professor Thomas had a smile all over his face and, with his eyes full of tears, he made a hand motion to invite him to come on stage.

The moment Daniel took his first step, he felt his father grabbed his upper arm. Daniel winced and looked at his father sitting next to him.

The father stood up, lowered his hand from Daniel's forearm to his palm, giving him a hand.

"Let's go together!", his father said. "You are my son and I am proud of you. You will never again have the feeling that you are walking through life alone!"

Daniel's face looked like the most beautiful sun had shone on it. His eyes shone like never before, and tears of happiness flowed down his cheeks.

"Let's go!", he said to his father, squeezing his hand even tighter as a sign of gratitude, but also of the strength his father had given to him. For the first time in his life, he walked proudly, next to his father, living his truth. It was the most beautiful moment he had ever experienced.

"Thank you, Dad!", Daniel said to his father, a moment before they climbed up the stage.

"Thank you, son! While I was trying to teach you how to live life, you taught me what life really is..."

Issa

The elevator doors opened and Issa rushed into the office.

That very second, the scent of her perfume spread throughout the office.

She looked flawless, as always. She wore a dress from the latest Moschino collection and Jimmy Choo shoes with dizzying heels. Today she chose a simple white purse from the fashion house Chanel. She always captivated with her appearance. After all, she invested a lot of attention in her appearance.

She was holding a cup of Starbucks coffee in her hand, as she did every morning.

With a determined step and a serious face, Issa walked towards her office. The sound of her heels could be heard by everyone in the editorial office. That's how they knew every morning that she had arrived. The energy of the entire editorial office would change instantly.

"Sophie, to my office!", she said, passing by her desk, without pausing.

Sophie stood up with a downcast look, knowing what this kind of invitation meant.

"Close the door!", Issa said in a bossy tone, setting her purse and coffee down on the table.

"Where is the article that was supposed to be in my email last night?"

Sophie stayed on her feet, keeping a decent distance from her desk.

"Well, I don't have it. The story has not been confirmed", Sophie answered quietly.

"Hellooooo! Earth is calling Sophia! Not confirmed?! What year did you get stuck in? Where there's smoke, there's fire. You confirm it. Invent a source that confirmed your story. Write that you talked to her close friend who confirmed the affair. Simple as that."

"But I didn't!", Sophie answered again naively.

"I know very well that you didn't talk to her close friend and that does not play any role for me. It doesn't matter if you did or not, the important thing is that the readers don't know this. What is the purpose of this portal, Sophie?", Issa continued, not allowing Sophie to reply.

"Well, to inform people", Sophie answered.

"No, Sophie! We left informing behind, back in the seventies. This is 2022! The point is to earn wages! You don't live on information, honey! You need money to live! More clicks, more money! What is not clear here?"

"So, you want me to invent the whole story?", Sophie asked her again.

"You won't completely invent it, because stories about her affair are already circulating in the city. You're just going to upgrade that story a bit and make it interesting."

"But if I write that I talked to someone and that it is now confirmed to be true, she can sue us."

"She can, but she won't. Public figures don't do that any longer. They realized that the judiciary system is so slow and expensive and that it is not worth wasting their time on courts. By the time the lawsuits are over, they spend more money than they would have won by suing. It's likely that when they see the story, they'll post on his social media and that'll be it. By then, we will already have hundreds of thousands of visits to our portal and everyone will be happy and satisfied. The story will be interesting for a few days and then it'll be replaced by a new one. It's more than obvious that you're new at this. You'll get used to it, don't worry. When you get your first salary, everything will become easier for you and you will understand how this world works. Now go back to your desk. I expect an article on my desk in an hour."

At that moment, Issa's cell phone rang.

"That would be all. Close the door behind you". Issa said, reaching for her cell phone from her purse.

Sophie left the office with her head down.

"Amateurs!", she said out loud, bringing the cell phone closer to his ear.

"Hello, Emma", Issa answered, seeing her friend's name on the screen.

"Morning, my dear! Are you excited about tonight?", her friend asked her with a laugh.

"I can't even think about it", Issa answered.

"Last night I was in the office until eight, came home, jumped in the bath and fell asleep already at ten. When are we meeting?"

"I'll pick you up at eight fifteen. Robert and Eric will come to the restaurant at nine thirty. Get ready, he's very handsome. Robert and Eric have recently been working together on a project and Robert is sure that Eric is your type of guy. I haven't met him yet either, but I've seen him on photos. He's such a handsome guy, Issa. This could be it!"

"Take it easy, Emma! You know my opinion on men. You can't be careful enough. Maybe that's why I'm not particularly excited because I'm already prepared for disappointment. It's hard to find a normal guy today. You know how much everyone is afraid of strong women and in the beginning everything is like great, and then their complexes start to come out and who gets hurt?! Of course, a woman! A woman who ends up hurt only because she is capable and knows who she is and what she wants."

"Not everyone is the same, Issa!", Emma tried to improve the course of the conversation.

"If nothing else, we shall eat something and drink a glass of good wine."

"Yes," Issa said, exhaling deeply as she remembered all the previous times when, for the umpteenth time, excitement had turned to disappointment.

"I have to go now, I have a lot of work to do!", Issa greeted her friend.

"OK! See you at eight at your place. Think positive", Emma added at the end of the conversation.

The work day was chaotic for Issa, like many others. She had to supervise the work of the others in the editorial office on a daily basis because no one knew better than her how to run the portal. She raised it in one year, from zero to one of the most read portals in the country.

And she was changing on the way. She had to listen to the readers and find out what interests them the most. She herself went into that world altruistically, believing that she would be able to change something, but that world, however, changed her. You cannot survive if you do not become like others. She herself saw that, if they published an inspiring story about someone's business or scientific successes, the article would have several hundred views. If they invaded someone's private life, there would be an explosion of visits to the portal.

And the math is simple. More visits, more views. More views, more ads. More ads, more money. One does not live on air and good news, but on money.

She quickly realized and adapted to this fact.

She looked at the clock and saw that it was already half past seven. She had to head home, if she wanted to make it in time to get ready for dinner and the blind date arranged by Ema and Robert.

Ema has been with Robert for several years and he proposed to her in Santorini last summer. They were a great couple. Robert wasn't

Issa's type of man, but who was? And the man she married at the age of 25 turned out to be completely different than when they met. He had been cheating on her with a work colleague for the past several years. Issa had no idea about it. She trusted him endlessly and when she found out, she was still in denial for a long time and believed him that it wasn't true. Unfortunately, it was and that truth devastated her. After that, she didn't find anyone to whom she could trust. She used to go out on dates, but she would end them very quickly. She didn't trust men any longer and she would leave them after a move that she didn't like or that would arouse her suspicion.

Tonight, Ema and Robert want to introduce her to Eric. Allegedly, a very handsome man, who is also divorced. She will leave because she hasn't been on a date in a long time, but without any expectations.

She took a shower, poured herself a glass of wine, which she drank while choosing what to wear. She opted for a simple black Dior dress with one bare shoulder, red Dior heels and red lipstick. She cared a lot about her appearance and everything about her was expensive. She always got into arguments when someone said that the suit does not make the man. It certainly does, she said. You are what you wear. Clothes are your identity card, they define you, were the words by which she was recognizable. She heard the sound of a message on her cell phone.

I'm in front, Emma wrote to her.

She took the last sip of wine, looked in the mirror once more, satisfied with what she saw, took her purse, put her coat over her and went out.

They arrived at the restaurant a few minutes after nine thirty. As the waiter led them to the table, Issa felt a thrill. She saw him halfway through the restaurant. He was laughing, loudly revealing his beautiful white teeth. He was dressed in an impeccably stylish white shirt and jacket. In the next moment, their eyes met. His gaze made Issa's body tingle. He slowly began to stand up to meet her like a gentleman. He was still looking directly into her eyes, without looking down. Issa, unlike Eric, looked down. She doesn't even know why. She doesn't remember that ever happening to her. But she felt great. Somehow inexplicable.

"Good evening, guys!", Ema exclaimed in a cheerful tone, hugging Robert.

"Good evening, ladies!", Robert replied, kissing Emma on the cheek.

"Issa, this is Eric!", Robert continued, pointing at him.

"Good evening!", Issa said, extending her hand to Eric.

"Good evening, Issa!", Eric answered in a deep voice, gently squeezing her hand.

There was something inexplicable about his appearance.

Issa had the feeling that she hadn't met such a man in a long time. Masculine strength emanated from him in an incredible combination with tenderness. He was different from the other men she knew. Dark brown hair, a beard enough to emphasize his masculinity, and yet visibly groomed. Well-groomed face and beautiful brown eyes. He smelled really good. By the way, Issa loved it. She always said that a man should smell like a man. That there is nothing sexier to her than a man who leaves behind a scent trail. He had a gentleness in his eyes. He was different from the men Issa liked. She always "fell" for bad boys. And was always hurt along the way.

From the very beginning, she took her defensive stance, because it no longer occurs to her that another man would hurt her in her life. She promised that to herself.

The evening was great, with lots of laughs, fantastic food, and several bottles of quality wine. When it was time to leave, Emma turned to Issa:

"Honey, would you mind if Eric drove you home?"

"I wouldn't, of course!", Issa replied, aware of Emma's plan to bring them together from the beginning of the evening.

Ride with Eric was pleasant. He told her how he met Robert at the car show in Prague and how they instantly became friends, and not long after that they started a business collaboration. He didn't reveal much about himself, which Issa liked. She liked his secrecy and the amount of moderation he had on the first date.

When they arrived in front of her house, he turned off

the car and went outside to open the door for her. He held out his hand as he got out of the car, and Issa, for the second time tonight, looked down, feeling like a little girl.

They stood opposite each other, now looking into each other's eyes.

"Thank you for the wonderful company tonight,", Eric addressed her with a smile.

"Thank you, Eric", Issa answered.

"I will be so free to ask for your number. I would like to see you again."

"Sure", Issa replied, taking her business card out of her purse and handing it to him.

Eric took the business card, gently touching her hand. Unobtrusively, he leaned towards her and kissed her on the cheek. "Good night, Issa. Talk to you soon."

"Good night, Eric!" she replied, quietly walking towards the door of the house.

Eric stood still, watching her, until she closed the door behind her.

Issa could hear the sound of the engine of Eric's car driving away from the house.

She felt her heart beat faster and her breathing quicken.

She sat down on a small cabinet in the hallway, trying to pull herself together after everything that had just happened.

She was overjoyed that he didn't try to kiss her because she doesn't believe she would agree to a kiss, and yet she seemed to be thinking about what kind of kiss it would be.

Okay, Issa, stop it!, she said out loud. Don't get carried away. They are all wonderful at first date. Then they turn into nightmares. No one will play that game with me again. Done!, she said proudly, standing up and taking off her coat and shoes.

She poured herself another glass of wine and headed for the bathroom.

Tomorrow is Saturday and she is not going to the office. She will relax in the tub and sleep as much as her heart desires.

She lay down in the bathtub, preparing to enjoy the silence, from which she was suddenly startled by the sound of a message.

She reached for her cell phone that was next to the bathtub and saw a message from an unknown number.

Thank you once again for a wonderful evening. I enjoyed your company immensely. If you have even thought of me for even one second since we parted, I will consider that it was pleasant for you, too. Please, if my messages make you uncomfortable in any way, feel free to tell me, and I will prepare in advance that such a message will not come from you, because I believe that you also think that our time has just begun. Eric

Issa stared at the message, not blinking or breathing. Again, she felt the excitement she didn't want to feel. He surprised her again with his completely unexpected action. He texted her 30 minutes after they separated. She was trying to remember if she had ever experienced this from a man before and of course she hadn't. Not only that she hadn't, but she always had to wait a few days for a man to contact her after the first date. Later she realized that it was a game played by alpha males who don't care and try to make a woman think about them and wonder if they will answer. She was used to that game. Not to a man like this one.

She wondered what to do now? To reply to him or not? This game was unknown to her.

She decided not to reply to him. She'll let him think she fell asleep.

It's time for someone to wait for me, she thought, putting her cell phone aside.

She was lying in the bathtub, with countless thoughts in her head. She felt worse and sadder. All the pains she went through with her ex-husband and the men after him were going through her head. She always just wanted to be loved and live love, but she was never able to do that. Tears ran down her cheeks and she began to cry loudly. It was as if the pain she felt became unbearable and she had to get it out of her.

My God!, she exclaimed, through tears.

If you can hear me, please help me. Help me not to be hurt anymore and to recognize in time what is for me and what is not. If you are there, now is the time for you to be there for me.

She said these words, while wiping the tears from her face.

And that requires a miracle!, she said in a sarcastic tone, exhaling deeply and diving completely into the tub.

Issa was still in bed when she heard the doorbell ring.

She took the cell phone that was on the bedside table and saw that it was ten o'clock.

Who is it now, in the middle of a Saturday morning?!, she thought. She got up, put on her dressing gown, slipped her cell phone into her pocket, put on her slippers and went down the stairs to open the door.

When she opened the door, she saw an elderly man, about eighty years old.

"What do you want?," she asked impatiently and angrily.

"Good morning! I apologize. I just moved here and I don't have anything in the house yet. Would you be so kind as to give me some sugar so that I can drink my tea?", the man asked.

"Sir, you woke me up, and on one of the rare days when I can sleep as much as I want", answered Issa gruffly, closing the door in his face without saying goodbye.

Visibly annoyed, she headed back upstairs, when she heard the bell ring again.

She opened the door again, even more nervous than a

moment ago, and again saw the same man at the door.

"I'm Tallis", the old man said calmly, as if Issa had opened the door for him for the first time.

"I moved into the house opposite yours. Excuse me, if I bother you, would you be so kind as to give me some sugar so that I can have my morning tea?"

Issa couldn't believe what was happening. Doesn't this man realize that he's bothering her?! She never thought of getting to know her neighbours and she has been maintaining superficial good-neighbourly relations for years. She didn't have time for neighbours.

"Try at someone else's house", she said rudely, closing the door again.

This time she did not head towards the room and waited to see if the bell would ring again. As a few moments passed and it didn't happen, Issa moved closer to the window and saw the old man crossing the road and entering the house directly opposite hers.

That house stood empty for a long time. She didn't even know that someone had moved in. The old man entered the house, closing the door behind him.

Finally, Issa thought, now wide awake. There is no point in going back to bed, she thought and went to the kitchen to make herself some coffee.

He heard the doorbell ring again. She was furious now. She

grabbed the door handle and while opening it, she was already speaking furiously: "Are you out of your mind?!"

At the door, she saw the same man again, who was now holding two cups in his hands.

"Good morning", he said in a completely calm voice, again as if seeing her for the first time.

"I am Tallis. I moved into the house opposite you yesterday.

Are you free for a morning tea? The tea is ready, we just need to add a little sugar."

Issa couldn't believe what she was witnessing. Did this man escape from the asylum? What doesn't he understand?

"Sir!" she said angrily.

"I'm not for tea, and especially not with you!"

"That's exactly what you need today", the man answered in a calm voice.

"Come again? What does that mean?", Issa asked him.

"That you really need to talk to someone", the man answered.

"What are you talking about, who are you?"

"Someone who sees your pain. Who sees the walls you built, thinking that you will protect yourself, not realizing that you built the pain on your side of the wall."

Issa was speechless. She was looking at this man with grey hair and deep blue eyes. He wasn't dangerous, quite the opposite. He looked benign and timid. And yet he radiated incredible strength and wisdom. Issa remained speechless, trying to process what she had just heard.

The man continued: "Take my word for it. Have tea with me. You don't even realize how much you need it right now. I see who you are. I know who you are."

Issa didn't know what to say. She felt herself surrender. She opened the door wide, motioning for this man to enter.

Tallis walked into the house and sat down on the couch.

Issa was still standing by the door, completely confused by the scene she was just witnessing.

"Can I have that sugar now?", Tallis addressed her with a smile.

Issa went to get sugar and a teaspoon and brought them into the living room. She placed them on the coffee table and sat down on the sofa opposite Tallis, still not saying a word.

Issa was still completely confused. She couldn't explain to herself why she let this man into the house, and again, it was as if it was stronger than her.

Putting sugar in the tea, Tallis looked at her, smiled gently and said:

"Issa, are you a happy woman?"

Issa was confused. He knew her name, and probably a lot more than that. She couldn't fight any longer, neither with him nor with herself. She decided to surrender to this unusual moment, counting on the fact that it would end faster that way.

"Of course, I'm happy. What kind of question is that?!", she answered nervously, putting sugar in her tea in order not to hide her nervousness because she instantly remembered her tears last night in the bathtub.

"How do you know you're happy?", Tallis asked her again.

"Because I have everything I wanted and I can afford everything I want," Issa answered.

"And what if you run out of it?"

What is this man talking about, what kind of questions are these?, she thought to herself.

"Why would I run out of it?"

"Because it's possible, right? Don't you know people who have experienced this? That once in their life they were at the top, and then, due to a combination of circumstances, they fell to the bottom?"

"Well, yes, of course I know them, but what does that have to do with me?! It can't happen to me."

"Anything can happen, Issa! Life is unpredictable and that's exactly the beauty of it."

"Well, let's say it can happen to me. And what about that?"

"Would you still be happy?"

"Well, of course, I wouldn't be happy if I was left without

everything I have."

"Exactly! You think you are happy now because you think happiness is in what you have. Listen to yourself what you said. You are happy because you have, because you own something. And if you stay without it, you wouldn't be happy any longer. You think that happiness is in having, owning. And that's why you're not really happy at all."

Issa did not like this conversation. Who does this man think he is? What gives him the right to ask her such questions and tell her that she is not happy.

"When was the last time you cried?", Tallis continued with questions.

Issa looked at him, trying to figure out if this man was reading her thoughts and how he knew how sad she was the last night. Should she lie to him? What should she do?

"I don't cry," she replied, looking down.

"Tears are for weak people."

"Uh, how inaccurate that is", Tallis replied, sipping some more tea.

"Tears are the expression of our soul. And only strong people are in touch with it. Do you know how much courage it takes to see deep inside and lay bare in front of our soul. Vulnerability is a reflection of strength. The strongest people are those who are not afraid to be vulnerable. But their strength is manifested precisely in their ability to grow and become strong through vulnerability. You were vulnerable last night too, weren't you?"

Issa was completely shocked. Is this man reading her thoughts? How did he know she cried in the tub last night?

Issa looked at him, not answering.

"Issa, trust me. Just trust me", Tallis said in a voice full of tenderness.

"Stop fighting. Both with me and yourself. Relax. Relax and let go, nothing bad will happen to you. Look at me as your best friend right now because I am that. I know you still don't understand what's going on, but now you need to listen to your heart. You listened to it the moment you let me in. You listened to your heart because your mind closed the door on me twice. Your heart let me in. Listen to your heart now, too. What is your heart telling you?"

The tears started rolling down Issa's cheeks when she heard these words. She couldn't stop them. Oh, how these words hit her. At this moment, this unknown man reminded her of her dad, whom she missed so much. Only her dad knew to talk to her like this. Only he saw her heart and always told her to listen to it. But he hasn't been around since Issa was twenty. One morning he was simply gone. Returning from the store early in the morning, he suffered a heart attack in front of their house. Issa was sleeping at the time and they didn't let her see him afterwards. Her dad's last words to her the night before were to follow and listen to her heart. And his heart betrayed him. That day changed Issa, and from that day on, she wanted absolutely nothing to do with her heart.

Issa was still crying. Tallis let her to cry. He knew that tears rinse the soul and are always healing.

"I stopped listening to my heart a long time ago", Issa replied through tears.

"I don't trust my heart because it was the heart that failed my father. The most wonderful man in the world who always thought of everything and everybody but himself. If the heart was honest, my dad would still be alive."

"And what if it was precisely because he gave himself so much to everyone that he wore out his heart?", Tallis asked.

Issa looked at him, as if she was telling him that she didn't understand what he was saying.

"You know how people often say that God is unfair because, if God were fair, good people would not die. And they often wonder how it is possible that people who think of everything, except themselves, die of various diseases or heart attacks?"

"Yes, that is exactly my question."

"Because such people forget about themselves. And self-love is the most important thing for a happy heart. We live in a world where people call good people those who constantly give themselves to others and don't know how to say *no*. And that, in fact, is the exploitation of people. There isn't a person who doesn't feel like saying *no* to others at some point. But people who forgot themselves also forgot how to say *no*. And so, they tell everyone that they do everything others ask them to do, give themselves one hundred percent to others and completely neglect themselves, their desires, their joys and everything that would truly make them happy. And so, they forget about their heart. Every time they say *yes* to others, they say *no* to themselves. And that's how the heart is wasted. It withers."

Issa listened to him, as if she were under hypnosis. She had never thought this way. And so, everything she heard now makes sense. And she felt Tallis was right.

Tallis let her go in silence again for a while. He knew that she was sorting her thoughts out, which were being agitated at the moment. He knew what it's like when people find out for the first time that there is a different way of looking at life. In that moment, their deep convictions on the subject show crystal clear to them, and it takes time for the mist that has been in front of their eyes for many years to burst.

"I don't know what my heart is telling me", Issa answered quietly. "I stopped listening to it."

"Go back to it, Issa!. Your heart never stopped talking to you. Your mind overpowered him. The more you silence your mind, the more clearly you will hear your heart. What dialogue is going on in you right now, Issa? Tell me about it."

Issa was now ready to completely surrender to this conversation.

"My mind keeps telling me that I'm not normal for letting

you into my house. And what am I doing here now and why am I even sitting with you, and at the same time I feel like I should. Ever since you sat down with me, it's as if something is pulling me to you and this conversation. I can't really explain it. It's as if I know deep down that your intentions are noble, and at the same time I'm confused by this moment, which is not quite normal."

"Right!", Tallis answered her, clapping his hands.

"That's it. You see how the dialogue between heart and mind is going on inside you all the time. Just to clarify something. When I say heart, I don't mean an organ. Let's be realistic, the heart is just an organ, like the liver, kidneys and brain. He doesn't have any magical powers. But it is a very important organ. Because it's the first organ showing us that life has begun and when it stops working, our life ends. When I tell you listen to your heart, I mean your soul. To that whole set of emotions that make you a human being with empathy and feelings. Do you understand that?"

"Yes, I understand."

"In order to truly understand life, you need to learn to listen to both the mind and the heart. Because the mind is not always wrong. The most important thing is to find a balance between these two. To distinguish when the mind is right and when it's not. I could have really been some madman who wanted to enter your house and do who knows what to you, but then you wouldn't have had this dialogue of heart and mind. Do you understand? If that were the case, your heart would know it and not respond. Let's go back to my question from a while ago, and you'll see what those dialogues look like. Did you cry last night?"

"Yes", Issa replied, looking down. "And, can you tell me why you were crying?"

Issa was silent for a few moments, as if trying to remember the exact reason.

"Everything came to me at once. Last night I met a wonderful man who didn't say a wrong sentence the whole evening, who behaved like a real gentleman, who sent me a wonderful message last night right after we parted our ways, and I didn't reply to him out of fear. I cried because I remembered all those times when I believed in love and gave my all, but always ended up being hurt. That's why I cried. Because I want to love and be loved, but I'm afraid to surrender to love. I'm simply scared."

Issa said the last sentence with a soft breath, as if it was a breath of relief because she had finally said everything that had been bothering her for a long time.

"What is it that you are afraid of?", Tallis asked.

"I'm afraid to get hurt again."

"Do you know why you are afraid?"

"I know! Because I've already experienced it."

"No! You're scaring yourself!"

"What do you mean? I don't scare myself. I'm afraid that what happened to me before will happen to me again. The thought of trusting someone again and having that someone hurt me scares me."

"Come on, stop for a moment! Simply stop everything. Just breathe and look into my eyes."

Issa took a deep breath and looked Tallis straight in the eyes.

"Clear your head of all thoughts. Just look at me. Try not to think about me, even though you're looking at me. Don't jump to conclusions about my hair, skin colour, eyes, etc. Just look at me, without a single thought."

Issa was trying to do as he told her. How could he know that she immediately began to think about what she saw. How could she not conclude that he has grey hair when she looks at him.

"Just look at me!", Tallis continued.

"Yes, some thought about me will come to you, but recognize it and put it away. Just let it go away. Don't fight it. Notice it and let go- Don't hold on to it And especially bring awareness to moments without thoughts. When you feel that you are just looking and existing."

Issa obeyed him. She was looking into his eyes, noticing her thoughts. God, how many thoughts she had! She noticed thoughts about his hair, the colour of his eyes. About the wrinkles she saw, about his nostrils that flared as he breathed. About his lips, teeth, beard. And she did everything as he told her. She was noticing her thoughts. It was as if she was observing them.

Tallis was silent and just observed.

They stood like that for a while, when Tallis suddenly spoke: "Do you feel fear now?"

"No!"

"And why did you feel it five minutes ago and not now?"
"Well, this moment I have nothing to be afraid of."

"That's right! And why isn't there anything to be afraid of?"

"Because I'm looking at you and I don't think about anything."

"Exactly! You're not thinking. And if you start thinking about Eric now, will you be afraid again?"

"Probably."

"But, why?"

"Because whenever I think of Eric, I get scared."

"Incorrect!"

"How incorrect, when it is correct! As soon as I start thinking about nice moments with him, I start to feel bad and scared."

"It's not true, Issa! Because if you really thought about Eric and nice moments you had with him, you would feel wonderful. When you start thinking about Eric, you go out of the present moment – into the past or the future. It has nothing to do with

Eric. Eric stayed in the present. You left the present moment. Don't be afraid of Eric or love! Like I said, you're scaring yourself!"

"Explain it to me, please!"

"Fear is nothing but an emotion caused by thoughts. And it's an emotion we cause to ourselves. Here's an example. Are you afraid of any animals?"

"Yes, I'm afraid of dogs. When I was little, I was bitten by my neighbour's dog, and since then, whenever I see a dog, I feel fear."

"OK, great! When you see a dog, you instantly go back in time. You remember yourself when you were a child and how you were bitten by a dog. Where do you go when you see a dog?"

"To the past."

"Exactly! Did you get bitten by the dog you saw yesterday?"

"No."

"And yet you felt fear, didn't you?"

"Yes!"

"You see, that dog doesn't scare you. You scared yourself, leaving the present moment and returning to the past. And because of that past, you also go into the future because you imagine a scene in which this dog attacks you in advance. Your past caused your thoughts about the future that never happened at all, and you lived them in yourself. Do you understand what

I'm trying to tell you? Your fear has nothing to do with the dog you see. Fear is a consequence of your thoughts when you see a dog. It's the same thing with Eric, too. When you think of him, you go to the past where you were hurt, and then you go to the future where Eric will do the same to you. And your fear has absolutely nothing to do with Eric. He suffers the consequences of your thoughts, not his actions."

Issa was silent. Tallis was right. Eric was wonderful to her yesterday. She really can't find any faults at the moment, and she treats him like he's already made a few missteps.

"What should I do?", Issa asked.

"Don't get out of the present moment. Especially not when it comes to love You said Eric texted you last night. Come on, answer him now!"

Issa reached into the pocket of her dressing gown and pulled out her cell phone.

"How did you really feel when you received his message and read it? Remember how you felt before your thoughts took you back in time."

"I felt beautiful. I felt special. And surprised because I'm not used to a man texting me the same evening after our first date. And the message was beautiful, moderate but full of feelings at the same time. He let me know that he really liked me and wanted to see me again."

"And what would you say to him with your heart?"

"I would tell him that I liked him a lot too and that it was wonderful of him to contact me right away. I would answer that it doesn't bother me at all."

"And are you going to answer him like that?"

"I don't think so. It doesn't work that way in love relationships."

"And how does it work, Issa?"

"Well, you have to be a little calculated. Play games. You shouldn't show that you care right away. If you show that you care, they disappear immediately."

"The wrong ones disappear, Issa. The ones you wouldn't be happy with. If you show your feelings to a man and he disappears, have you lost anything? Didn't he do you a favour by doing that? Didn't he show you right away that this is a man who doesn't know how to show his feelings?! How can you even think that you lost something there?!"

Tallis was right again, Issa thought. This man sees things completely differently from her.

"You can't lose when it comes to love, Issa. You may feel like you're losing something, but when you realize that you're only losing what wasn't love at all, you start to see things as they are. And that is that you don't lose anything. That you're always on gain. Either you get love or the realization that it's not love. If you send Eric a message from the heart, you'll immediately see what kind of message you'll get back. A lot of things will become clearer to you. And if the present moment with him is good for you, enjoy it. The present moment is all you truly have. People usually miss it. They live in thoughts and fears. And instead of being happy in the present moment, they live in calculated moments, always waiting for something. And that something they are waiting for will never come. Because they are already in what they are waiting for. And that is the present moment. Which they miss."

"Okay", Issa replied as she prepared to reply to Eric's message.

Tallis leaned back on the couch, sipping his tea.

They sat in silence for a few moments. Issa typed the message without stopping.

"Can I read it to you before I send it?", she asked shyly.

"Of course!"

Dear Eric, Thank you for your wonderful message. I fell asleep as soon as I got home last night, so I am replying to you now...

"Your mind has interfered again!", Tallis interrupted her.

Issa knew exactly why he said that. Yes, she lied to Eric about falling asleep, and she no longer even wondered how Tallis knew. Now she already knew that this strange man in her house was much more than an ordinary man.

"Okay", Issa said, deleting the message and typing again for a while in silence.

Dear Eric, Thank you for your wonderful message. You're not bothering me at all. In fact, I'm very happy that you wrote to me so soon. Nice of you. I really liked you too, and I'm certainly looking forward to seeing you again and the time ahead.

"Excellent!", Tallis told her with satisfaction.

"Now send it."

Issa took a deep breath and clicked the Send button.

"Sent!", she blurted out, unsure of what would happen next.

"I'm going now,", said Tallis, as he stood up.

"Shall we drink tea together again?" Issa asked him, as she got up to see him off.

"Of course, we will!", Tallis answered, giving her a gentle smile.

"Can I hug you?", Issa asked him.

Without a word, Tallis spread his arms and Issa hugged him tightly, with a lot of tenderness.

"Thank you, Tallis. Thank you for this."

"You're welcome, Issa. Didn't I tell you that you really needed this tea with me?"

"Yes, you did. And you were right again. I am very happy to have met you."

"See you soon!", Tallis said walking out of Issa's house.

"See you," Issa greeted him.

She remained standing in the doorway, watching Tallis cross the road and enter the house.

At that moment, she heard the sound of a message.

At the same moment, her heart began to beat excitedly because she thought that Eric had written to her.

She took the mobile phone and, looking at the screen, spread a smile across her face. It was Eric.

Dear Issa,

This Saturday morning has now become even more beautiful.

Thank you for replying to my message.

I'm free today, so I was wondering if you would like to go on a picnic in nature with me?

Issa was overjoyed. Sure, I would like to, she said it out loud and started laughing to herself. She did not allow her thoughts to stop or sabotage her. She will listen to her heart to see what will happen. She doesn't remember the last time she did that. What if that's the way? What if that's the only right way?

Dear Eric, sure! I would love to. I'm also free today and I'd love to go on a picnic with you. I can be ready in an hour

In a few moments there was a return message from Eric

Deal! I'll pick you up in an hour! I know where.

Where last night I kissed the most tender face in the world.

Issa melted. She felt like she was floating. She ran to her room to get ready.

Eric arrived to pick her up in exactly an hour. He waited by his car and when she got out, he went up to her and kissed her hand. Issa felt his irresistible scent again. He had a broad smile on his face and vibrated with wonderful energy.

"Ready?", Erik asked her, opening the car door for her.

"Ready!", replied Issa with a smile, looking at him seductively.

Her brain was racing. She could feel her heart beating again, but this time it felt different. She didn't let her mind sabotage her heart. She promised herself that she would listen to Tallis's words and not leave the present moment. Next to her was a beautiful man who, with not a single move, did anything that would indicate that she would be hurt. And she decided to stay there. In present. That's the only truth.

"Where are you taking me?", Issa asked him, tossing her hair aside and putting on her sunglasses.

"To a wonderful place. Do you trust me?"

"Yes!", Issa replied, sighing deeply as she truly felt the truth of her own words.

They drove for about thirty minutes and enjoyed talking about anything and everything.

Issa was getting more relaxed with every second.

They arrived at a beautiful open park, where Issa had never been.

When they got out of the car, Erik opened the trunk and took out the blanket and basket he had prepared for the picnic.

Issa was delighted. She always liked to feel led by a man. She loved feeling safe and that she could let herself go.

They found a wonderful place by the lake. Eric spread the blanket and opened the basket. A bottle of white wine, two glasses and some grapes and wonderful Italian cheese – these were the contents of the basket.

"Relax, miss", Eric told her, motioning for her to sit down while he served and prepared everything for them.

Issa took off her shoes and sat down. She didn't take the smile off her face. She enjoyed every moment with Eric.

Eric opened a bottle of wine and poured it into their glasses.

"So, let's make a toast!"

"To what?", Issa asked, knowing that Eric had picked up on her wiggly intent.

"To the future! But also, to this moment, which, I believe, will lead us there."

Issa was delighted again. How did he always know exactly what to say?

"Ask, Issa, relax and ask whatever you want."

"Whatever I want?"

"Yes, I suggest we start honestly from the very first second."

"Well, OK! How come you're alone?"

"That's how I chose until now. Because I don't want to settle for less than what I know I can have. When I realized that my ex-wife had a completely different view on life than I did, I decided that it was better for us to separate than to go through life full of resentment. Not only me, but she would also become bitter. I was becoming more and more dissatisfied, and such a person could not be the best husband, which I want to be. She would really feel it, and thus become more and more unhappy. And then we would fall into that vicious circle of two unhappy and frustrated people. We just weren't compatible, and the longer we were together, the more aware I was becoming of that fact. I'm someone who, for example, is never late, and lateness was her middle name. Every time, when I would wait for her for hours, I would become more and more frustrated and complain to her. She would tell me that being late is something normal and that the problem is with me. And there would be arguments. And so, day after day. I am very organized and ambitious, someone who wants to use all his potential and believes that he can, while she was content with little and never aspired to experience all the beauty that life has to offer. Every day looked the same to her. She slept until lunch, was awake until three in the morning, so we almost haven't seen each other. I wanted children, but it was too much of a responsibility for her and she thought she wouldn't be able to do it. And so on. It was simply better to end it than to suffer for the rest of your life, blaming each other. Or, God forbid, cheat on her. I would never allow myself to do that. I don't do to others what I don't want someone to do to me. When we got divorced, I promised myself that I will no longer agree to less than what I know is important to me in a partnership. I know exactly what views I want my future partner to have on life."

Issa was listening to him intently. She was delighted with his words and his view on life.

"And what is cheating for you?"

"Everything that the latter would not do if his partner was next to him!"

"Hallelujah!", Issa exclaimed and Eric started laughing loudly.

"That's exactly what I've been telling you all the time. To this day, my friends try to convince me that there are various types of cheating and that some of them are not really terrible, but I simply cannot accept that in a relationship. To me, cheating is exactly what you said. Everything I do, but wouldn't want my partner to be there. Amen. There are no levels or species or subspecies."

"I agree", replied Eric, looking into her eyes gently, as if he was telling her with his eyes that he liked her way of thinking.

"Are you careful in love?". Eric asked her. "Um...", Issa began, remembering Tallis.

"I have to admit that I was, until yesterday. I myself was

cheated and deceived, so I became cautious. I swore to myself that no one would hurt me again. But I realized that if I approach love cautiously, how can I live love. I am tired of this constant thinking about my next action. Then I don't live with my heart, but with my mind. I would like to relax and surrender to love. I know deep down that love is beautiful and that if it hurts, it's not love."

Eric looked at her lovingly. He liked that she opened up to him and showed him how vulnerable she was.

They talked for two hours, without any calculation, both completely open to perhaps even today realizing that they are not for each other. But that didn't happen. The more they talked, the more certain they were that they had found another part of themselves.

Issa had Tallis's words in her head all the time and could accurately recognize the dialogue between mind and heart. And every time her mind tried to sabotage her; her heart managed to silence it. She doesn't remember ever having such an honest and open conversation with a man.

With each minute passing by, she liked Eric more and more. She had never met such an honest, vulnerable and, at the same time, strong man. Again, she remembered Tallis's words that vulnerability is an expression of the greatest strength, and she could see that strength in Eric.

"Issa," Eric continued, taking her palms in his.

"I am here with you today only because of one wish. Wish

to live love. I am someone who does not play games, who would rather love and be hurt a hundred times than someone who will never love. How will we know if the person is right for us, if we are not who we really are. It is not the end of the world to understand that people are different and not compatible. It would be the end of the world for me not to try. Let's indulge in it, Issa! Let's enjoy every moment without brakes, calculations, trips to the past and the distant future. Let's stay in the present and see what happens. What do you say? Will you be my girl that I will love madly, be honest with her, see the most beautiful part of her at every moment and always say how I feel, listening to your feelings at the same time. Will you be my best friend and girlfriend at the same time?"

Issa looked at him without blinking. She couldn't believe what she was hearing. She had never experienced a man say such words to her. With each of his next sentences, Issa fell more and more in love with him.

"Oh, how I'd like that, Eric!", Issa said, still looking into his eyes.

"I would like that more than anything."

At that moment Eric put his hands on her cheeks, without taking his eyes off her eyes, he brought his lips to hers and kissed her softly. Issa felt the most beautiful warmth taking over her entire body. She could literally feel herself melting. It was as if all the walls she had built collapsed at the same time and only her was left, naked and barefoot in front of love. And she felt free. She felt like a woman, after a long time. Vulnerable and strong at the same time. It was the most beautiful kiss she had ever experienced.

They spent the whole weekend together at Eric's house. They endlessly enjoyed each other, talking about anything and everything. About life, work, friendships, wishes, ambitions and dreams. They talked about the future, without leaving the present moment. They made love for hours. They watched movies together, delighted that they had the same taste in genres, laughed out loud and were more and more in love with each other every minute of the day, more and more sure that they both found what they were looking for.

Monday started dramatically, as most of Issa's Mondays. She drove to work angry as hell. As soon as she opened her eyes this morning, she saw that a competing portal had published a bombastic story about a famous athlete with a video of him kissing an unknown girl in a night club, while his pregnant wife was in the maternity hospital being monitored for pregnancy. She went mad because she didn't understand how they didn't find out about that story first.

Stepping out of the elevator, she immediately shouted: "Everyone to the meeting room. Immediately!"

The entire editorial team gathered in the room. No one dared to speak. Issa was standing on her feet at the back of the table, leaning on her palms. It was clear to everyone from her body language and look that she was as angry as hell.

"I will not say good morning to you, because the morning is not good at all. It's even worse when I realize that I work with a bunch of incompetent people who can't see what's in front of their noses. Can someone explain to me how it is possible that we could not publish the story, which will be the most striking news for days now?"

Everyone was silent.

"Okay. Sophie, I hold you the most responsible.

Please pick up your things and leave the office."

"What?!", Sophie exclaimed in disbelief. "Are you firing me?"

"Yes, which part isn't clear to you? You are incompetent and useless. You were already on thin ice on Friday, when I had to remind you how to do this job and now this. I think that would be it."

"But this is not our fault, and even less mine. The video was sent to the portal last night by their reader. And published this morning. How could we come up with the story, if the story did not exist until this morning?"

"Sophie, you can head for the exit", Issa continued coldly. "We're done," said Issa, picking up her purse from the table and walking out of the editorial office.

Issa got into the car and headed home. He can't be in the office today.

She felt how angry and nervous she was and it was better, both for her and for everyone else, to stay away from people.

She parked in front of her house, when she saw Tallis sitting on the porch of his house.

"Good morning, Issa!", Tallis shouted to her, waving cheerfully.

"How are you this morning, on this beautiful day?"

"It's a really beautiful day, it couldn't be better," replied Issa grimly, crossing the road towards him.

"So, a perfect day for our tea."

Issa pulled up a chair and sat next to him.

"I'll agree on everything, as long as I get away from people because it seems to me that I could kill someone."

"Oops!", Tallis replied, getting up to bring her a cup of tea. "There you go, Issa", he said in a few moments, when he returned.

"Let me hear, why did you put yourself in that state?"

"Me, myself? I didn't put myself in that state, but incompetent people put me there. I had a wonderful weekend with Eric. It couldn't be more beautiful, and then this morning, as soon as I opened my eyes, I saw that my incompetent people had missed to disclose the most striking news of the day, and as it seems to me, this will also be the news of the month. There won't be a person who won't click on these news today, and do you know how much money that will cost me. Incompetent people just cost me thousands of Euro. Therefore, I did not bring myself to this state, but those who work for me."

"And how exactly are they to blame?"

"The video should have been sent to our editorial office, but it wasn't." "And why not?"

"Because. The reader decided to go to another portal, which is our biggest competitor."

"So, if the reader has made up his mind, what does that have to do with your staff?"

"Well, they should have done something to send the video to us."

"And why didn't you do something? Why didn't you do what you required of them?"

"Well, it seems to me that I'm the only one doing quality work."

"And what exactly, Issa, could they have done yesterday for you to publish the story? Or let's be even more precise, what exactly would you have done yesterday so that you would have published the story?"

Issa fell silent. At that moment, she realized the insanity of her words. What would she do? Well, nothing. Because she couldn't do anything. No one could have guessed what would happen the last night in the club. A person who happened to be there recorded the situation and sent the video the same evening. No one had any idea that this video would be posted this morning.

"Yes, I couldn't do anything", she said quietly.

"Then why are you asking your employees to do something that you yourself couldn't do."

Issa didn't answer.

"Rage just blinded you, Issa. And you were so angry that you looked for relief in the wrong place. Why are you really angry?"

"I don't know..."

"Come on, find out! Find an answer because if you don't, the rage will become a part of your everyday life. Rage doesn't come by itself. It is an accumulated anger. If you don't deal with the feeling of anger right at the beginning, it turns into rage. What exactly has been making you angry for a long time, and you won't admit it to yourself?"

Issa was silent, but not because she didn't want to answer, but as if she was digging deep inside herself to come up with an answer.

"Do you want me to help you with this one?", Talis asked her.

"Sure!", Issa answered quietly.

"Do you wake up with excitement every Monday?"

"No, of course!"

"Why did you say of course?"

"Well, because Monday is not for me to wake up happy and excited, but to go to work, roll up my sleeves and start fighting problems and fighting for existence."

"Really? Is that what Monday is for? Really? I did not know that. What about other days of the week?"

"Well, the same. The only days when I can rest a little are Saturday and Sunday. And it's not even Sunday because I'm already partially stressed and preparing for Monday."

"Aha! So, out of seven days a week, we have one day to be happy and relaxed?!"

"Well, yes! Life is not made for us to be happy, but to survive it as best as we know how."

"Who taught you that?"

"Well, life has taught me. Everyone is struggling."

"And what if your life is like that because you believe it has to be like that?"

"I don't understand."

"Life isn't meant to be like that, Issa! It is conceived as a wonderful adventure that we will enjoy. In which we will love those we love to love and those who will love us. In which we will feel the most beautiful possible form of partner love. In which we will understand people and why they behave the way they do. In which we will do what we love and make a living of it. It is meant for us to wake up happy and excited every day in joyful anticipation of everything that lies ahead. Life is meant to be the ease of living."

"That's impossible, Tallis! Life is not a fairy tale or a love movie. Life is much more complicated. Full of pain and renunciation."

"And what if it's not like that?"

"But it is!"

"And what if it isn't? What if life is a reflection of what you believe life to be?"

"But, Tallis, I know what I see around me. And how other people live. One 'what if' can't deny the truth!"

"Truth is a very relative term, dear Issa! And yes, for you, everything you see around you is true, but you don't see the other truths."

"Other truths?"

"Yes, other truths. You only have access to what you deeply believe to be true. Truth is a result of what you believe in. And yes, it's true. I do not dispute your truth, but there are others. You can change the truth."

"How?!"

"For starters, stop calling it the only truth. Learn that truth is created by observing something and constantly confirming that it is so. That's how you cement what you observe into your reality as something that can't be changed, and then you even call it fate.

If you don't like what you live and if you don't like your truth, you can change it. Do you have even a little faith in that?"

"Well, I don't really know what to tell you, I'm sceptical."

"And that's excellent news. Being a septic means not blindly believing someone because he said something, being a sceptic means questioning and looking for evidence about something. Sceptics usually become the biggest believers in the end because they got the evidence in the best possible way. Through experience."

"And how do you change your truth?"

"By choices you will make starting from today. In order for your life to change, you have to change something. You cannot make the same choices as yesterday and expect change. You're the one that has to change. In the same reality and truth that you currently live, you have to become different."

"How?"

"First, by way of thinking. A limited way of thinking leads to a limited life. People with an open mind, ready to step out of their comfort zone and logical thinking, live such magical and spectacular lives that you can't even imagine it at this moment. And it all started with their minds being limitless and spectacular. What is the first thing you would do if you were sure you would succeed? What different choices would you make today?" "I wish the story from the last night had come to us!"

"Really? Why?"

"Because then we would be the most visited portal!"

"And why is that important to you?"

"Because I would make fantastic money this month!"

"And why is that important to you?"

"When I have money, I have peace."

"So, you want peace, not the story?"

Issa fell silent. At that moment, she understood what Tallis wanted to tell her.

"Well, yes", she replied quietly. "Actually, yes. I want peace."

"And why do you put your peace in someone else's hands? Why do you follow the path of turbulence, hoping to find peace that way."

"What do you mean?"

"Does your work bring you peace? Does disclosing other people's private things bring you peace?"

"Well, I don't see it that way."

"But you should. You should always be able to be the other one. And before you do something, you should ask yourself what would happen if they did the same to you. How would you feel? If you ask yourself that question, you will immediately know the consequences of the choices you make. And how your actions affect the others. You are so focused on earning that you don't even realize how you get there. And that's why you lose your peace. You cannot live a life where you cause pain to others and live in peace. You simply can't There is something called karma and every action has its consequence. That's just the way it is. It cannot be avoided. And the more people you hurt along the way, the more situations you will experience in which you will be hurt yourself."

Issa bowed her head. Perhaps for the first time in a long, long time, she was ashamed of herself.

"You needn't be ashamed, Issa!", Tallis told her this, once again clearly seeing what she was going through.

"People always do the best they can. Condemning and blaming people does not lead to anything. Most certainly, not to a change. You acted as you knew or didn't know, but if you learn better and become aware of unconscious patterns, then your actions will be better. Right away. You're changing your choices.

Issa instantly remembered Sophie. The girl she put all the blame on and fired her this morning. She put herself in Sophie's skin for the first time. How does she feel now?! Who knows where she is now and what she is doing. She must be crying somewhere in anger or fear of the future, but also because of how Issa treated her this morning.

Tallis looked at her again as if he knew what she was thinking.

"Fix it. Remember! Other choices, Issa!"

Issa reached for her cell phone and dialled Sophie's number, and at that moment Tallis got up and entered the house for a few minutes, leaving Issa alone, knowing how big this moment was for her.

When he returned, Issa was staring into the distance.

"It's settled", she said in a gentle tone.

"I corrected the mistake."

"Nice of you! Just know that mistakes are not bad, if we grow after them. And what we call mistakes is just a process of growth and learning. There is no mistake that cannot be corrected once you realize it. And how do you feel now?"

"Calmer."

"You see, your choices lead to peace, not what the others will do. And how do you think that girl feels now?"

"Very happy! She cried and screamed with happiness. She said she understood me and didn't hold anything against me. That she knows I'm under stress and that she's doing the best she knows and can."

"Does the thought of how she feels right now make you feel good?"

"Yes."

"That's where we find peace, Issa. By questioning our actions and not making choices out of affect, fear or anger. When we stop, quiet our mind and allow ourselves to balance with the life energy within us, our actions will be completely different. Now I would like to ask you again: What choice would you make today, if you knew that you would have peace?"

"I would no longer run the portal the way it works now. Now I realize that I make the most money when I hurt people the most. And even though I've been functioning like that for years, I still haven't achieved the peace I'm constantly chasing. And now I realize that I will never achieve it this way."

"Be the change you want to see in the world, Issa! Be what you truly want to be. Don't adapt to a world that is mostly in chaos and people sleepwalking through life, living some distorted version of it. Let the world adapt to you. And it will. Quite enough to live happily and enjoy your work. Not everyone needs to understand you and not everyone needs to agree with you. There's plenty of everything for everyone. Create your own truth! And the most beautiful thing in this story is that you will then vibrate with abundance. And when you feel it and enjoy your work, haven't you achieved what you thought all along that money would bring you? You don't even realize that in that race for money, you've been emitting the vibration of lack the whole time. An abundance of peace, joy, love, lightness and financial abundance will be your next step. That is the law of the Universe! You don't even realize that in that race for money, you've been sending out the vibration of lack the whole time. The whole time you were in fear if the money would come that month. Of course, the journey was exhausting. Because the journey is not even intended that way. Tell yourself what kind of life you want to live and believe that it is possible. Make choices without fear of success. Because the success will come!

We fail when we doubt and struggle with life. Declare to yourself and to life that you will love and be loved, that you will serve others with love and be the best version of yourself, that you will live in financial abundance and freedom and that you will wake up every day with excitement! Declare it daily and just observe. Observe how the entire Universe reorganizes itself because of you and how you begin to live that truth!"

The tears streamed down Issa's cheeks. She wanted to hear these words so much. She wanted to receive consolation and a kind word in her life. She felt the power of Tallis's words with her entire being.

She jumped up from her chair and threw herself into his arms. She hugged Tallis tightly, expressing her gratitude, not only with her lips, but with her whole being.

Tallis held her, like his own daughter, in a tender embrace, being aware of the healing which she was experiencing at this moment.

The next morning, Issa was jolted out of sleep by the sound of a large truck and the screeching of children outside the house. She got up and went to the window, when she saw a large moving truck full of furniture and a family with small children entering the house across the street from where Tallis lived.

What's going on here? Who's moving in? Tallis lives there.

She grabbed her dressing gown, ran downstairs and out on the street Tallis lives there.

"Excuse me! Sorry, what's going on here?"

"Good morning, madam", she was greeted by a man who was obviously the head of the family moving in. "Is everything all right?"

"I don't understand what is happening? Who are you? My friend lives here."

"You got something wrong, madam. We bought this house six months ago and today we got the keys and we are just moving in."

"Impossible. I was still there yesterday, at my friend Tallis's."

"Ma'am, you're mistaken. No one has lived in this house for a year."

Issa didn't hear him again. She ran into the house, looking for Tallis in disbelief.

"Tallis, Tallis!", she shouted, running around the house.

The house was serenely empty. All the furniture was covered with white sheets, with visibly accumulated dust, as if no one had stayed in that house for a long time.

She entered the kitchen looking for a tea set.

She saw it on the small round kitchen table. And there was accumulated dust on it, as if it had not been used for a long time.

Issa was completely confused.

What's going on? We drank tea from it yesterday!

She was looking at the kettle in disbelief, when she saw a folded piece of white paper under the kettle.

Issa approached the coffee table, trembling. She picked up the dusty teapot and, opening the message, felt the endless love and warmth that embraced her soul and tears started to flow down her cheeks.

The message said:

My dear Issa!

The truth is what we deeply believe in.

And what we believe in what really exists.

Live your truth now

And listen and follow your heart...

Your friend,

Tallis

The most beautiful possible morning dawned. Her wedding day. Issa woke up in a beautiful room in Sienna, Tuscany. Both Eric and her knew that there wasn't more beautiful place in the world, where they would immortalize their love. Gentle and romantic, like all of Tuscany, a place from fairy tale. As their love.

Today she's getting married to a man who is so easy to love. Eric proposed to her six months ago at the place he had taken her on a picnic for the first time. She said *yes*, simultaneously laughing and crying with happiness and relief that they had found each other and that they both knew how much they were made for each other.

She got up, sat on the bed and thought about how happy she was. The last two years were the most beautiful ones in her life.

She completely reorganized the portal and the way they work. The portal became what she wanted it to be in the first days. An informative tool that will provide people with information that will make their lives easier and more beautiful. Only now did she realize how much people longed for such a place in the media to provide safe and inspiring information and comfort in this world where they are bombarded with fake news and negativity. This is exactly why the portal has maintained a high readership because people were looking for refreshments in the sea of negativities. She continued to write about famous people, but this time every piece of news came directly to her from these public figures, who also recognized that they would not be judged and that they could present their side of the story. That was even more interesting to people. Issa was overjoyed. She realized that Monday doesn't have to be a bad day, but quite the opposite. A day that marks the beginning of a new week and new opportunities. She no longer paid too much attention to branded clothes, realizing now how much self-worth she sought in it. She was still elegant and always dressed up, but now she knew that she wore the clothes, not that she was worth as her clothes.

Now she saw clearly how much her race to own the latest fashion pieces was her need to fill a void within herself. And the happier she was, the freer she was from being enslaved by things.

Love with Eric was more and more beautiful. She no longer went into the past and did not allow her fears to control her. She gave herself completely to him, and that's exactly why she received such love in return. She found a man who adored every part of her and she really got to know everything Tallis taught her. Love is meant to be lightness. Tallis was right. Life can be wonderful.

"Well, here is our pretty bride! It's time to put on your wedding dress! Ready?", Ema entered the room cheerfully, hugging her.

"Yes... Readier than I'll ever be."

Everything was ready for the ceremony to begin. The garden of the beautiful castle in Sienna was decorated with flowers in pastel colours. Issa stopped at the beginning of the path that led to Eric. Eric stood under a beautiful arch covered in flowers, surrounded by their witnesses. Issa's godmother Emma and his godfather Robert. They were responsible for the two of them meeting and there was no other possibility but for them to be the witnesses of their love. Eric gasped when he saw Issa. He didn't even hold back his tears. He looked at her lovingly, just like on the first day. At that moment, the first bars of her and Eric's song *From This Moment* came from the speakers.

Issa exhaled deeply and just as she was about to take the first step and walk towards the altar herself, she felt someone grab her under the arm.

"You don't think you'll go this way alone to your future husband, do you?" someone whispered in her ear, grabbing her under the arm.

Issa turned her head in surprise and saw Tallis!

"Taaaalliiiis!", exclaimed Issa, throwing herself into his arms.

"God, is this possible, can life be this beautiful?!", Issa said, leaning her cheek against his.

"It can, Issa. It certainly can. That's exactly how it was designed. It's time to go. Eric is waiting for you."

Issa wiped away her tears, flashed the biggest smile she's ever had, and walked with Tallis towards the altar.

Walking to the sounds of the most beautiful song, Issa felt like she was going to explode with happiness. She was surrounded by people she loves and who love her. In front of her was her future husband, a man with whom she lives the kind of love she has always dreamed of, and she is being led to the altar by the man who taught her to live life and without whom this moment would not exist. She felt endless gratitude for how this moment felt and the life she was living.

When they reached Eric, who held out his hand to receive her, Issa rested her cheek against Tallis's and softly whispered:

"It's true, Tallis. The truth is that we can change our truth.

Thank you for this valuable life lesson."

Tallis kisses her on the cheek and with a loving look, handing her over to Eric, whispers:

"Yes, my Issa…"

"Life is beautiful, when you know how to live it…"

www.ingramcontent.com/pod-product-compliance
Lightning Source LLC
Chambersburg PA
CBHW051303120626
46547CB00015B/2075